DARK DAYS IN GHANA

DARK DAYS IN GHANA

Kwame Nkrumah

PANAF
London

DARK DAYS IN GHANA

ISBN   0 90 1787 09 4

Panaf Books
75 Weston Street
London SE1 3RS

DEDICATION

*To Major General Barwah, Lieutenant S. Arthur
and Lieutenant M. Yeboah and all Ghanaians
killed and injured resisting the traitors of the
24th February 1966.*

Works by Kwame Nkrumah

Africa Must Unite
Axioms of Kwame Nkrumah
Class Struggle in Africa
Consciencism
Dark Days in Ghana
Ghana (Autobiography)
Handbook of Revolutionary Warfare
I Speak of Freedom
Neo-Colonialism
Revolutionary Path*
Rhodesia File*
The Struggle Continues*
Towards Colonial Freedom
Voice from Conakry
What I Mean by Positive Action

Pamphlets

Ghana; The Way Out
What I Mean by Positive Action
The Big Lie
Two Myths: The Myth of the "Third World"
                "African Socialism" Revisited
The Spectre of Black Power

* Published Posthumously

AUTHOR'S NOTE

Ghana's experience since 24th February 1966, costly but priceless, must be viewed in the context of the African Revolution as a whole.

It is with this in mind that I have written, in Conakry, about Ghana's "dark days" in the hope that publication of the facts may help to expose similar setbacks in other progressive independent African states.

Conakry, Guinea.

15th April 1968.

Letter to Kwame Nkrumah from
Richard Wright: *Black Power*
(London and New York, 1954)*

I say to you publicly and frankly: The burden of suffering
that must be borne, impose it upon *one* generation! Do not,
with the false kindness of the missionaries and business-men,
drag out this agony for another five hundred years while your
villages rot and your people's minds sink into the morass of
a subjective darkness . . . Be merciful by being stern! If I
lived under your regime, I'd ask for this hardness, this
coldness . . .

Make no mistake, Kwame, they are going to come at you
with words about democracy; you are going to be pinned to
the wall and warned about decency; plump-faced men will
mumble academic phrases about "sound" development;
gentlemen of the cloth will speak unctuously of values and
standards; in short, a barrage of concentrated arguments will
be hurled at you to persuade you to temper the pace and drive
of your movement . . .

But you know as well as I do that the logic of your actions
is being determined by the conditions of the lives of your
people . . .

There will be no way to avoid a degree of suffering, of trial,
of tribulation; suffering comes to all people, but you have
within your power the means to make this suffering of your
people meaningful, to redeem whatever stresses and strains
may come. None but Africans can perform this for Africa.
And, as you launch your bold programmes, as you call on
your people for sacrifices, you can be confident that there are
free men beyond the continent of Africa who see deeply
enough into life to know and understand what you *must* do,
what you *must* impose . . .

* This extract is reproduced by the kind permission of the author's
London agents, John Farquharson Ltd., and of Harper and Row,
New York.

CONTENTS

I

PEKING TO CONAKRY

The word "coup" should not be used to describe what took place in Ghana on 24th February 1966. On that day, Ghana was captured by traitors among the army and police who were inspired and helped by neo-colonialists and certain reactionary elements among our own population. It was an act of aggression, an "invasion", planned to take place in my absence and to be maintained by force. Seldom in history has a more cowardly and criminally stupid attempt been made to destroy the independence of a nation.

When the action took place, I was on my way to Hanoi, at the invitation of President Ho Chi Minh, with proposals for ending the war in Vietnam. I had almost reached Peking, the furthest point in my journey. The cowards who seized power by force of arms behind my back, knew they did not have the support of the people of Ghana, and therefore thought it safer to wait until I was not only out of the country, but well beyond the range of a quick return.

The news was brought to me by the Chinese Ambassador in Accra who had gone on ahead to Peking to meet me, and to be with me during my visit to China. He had just accompanied Prime Minister Chou En-lai, Liu Shao-chi and other officials when they welcomed us at the airport, and he had come straight on out to the government house where I was staying. I remember his exact words:

"Mr. President, I have bad news. There has been a coup d'état in Ghana."

I was taking a brief rest after the long flight from Rangoon, and wondered if I had heard him correctly.

"What did you say?"
"A coup d'état in Ghana."

9

> "Impossible," I said. "But yes, it *is* possible. These things do happen. They are in the nature of the revolutionary struggle."

I learned later that the Chinese welcoming party had known about events in Ghana when I stepped from the aircraft at Peking, but with characteristic courtesy had waited to break the news to me privately.

My first reaction was to return immediately to Accra. If the VC10 of Ghana Airways in which we had travelled most of the way had been at Peking I would have embarked at once. But we had left it behind in Rangoon and had continued to Peking in an aircraft sent by the Chinese government.

I knew that to avoid unnecessary bloodshed I would have to be back in Ghana within 24 hours, and this was clearly impossible. I decided, therefore, to make an immediate statement to the Ghanaian people, and to fight back on African soil just as soon as my hosts could make the necessary travel arrangements.

What had happened in Ghana was no more than a tactical set-back in the African revolutionary struggle of a type which I had often predicted. At the very first conference of the O.A.U. in Addis Ababa, I had warned my fellow Heads of State that none of us was safe if we remained disunited. For this reason, I considered that the overall strategy remained unchanged but what had happened in Ghana made it all the more necessary to press on by revolutionary means to secure a united Africa.

The following is the text of the statement I released to the press:

> "On my arrival in Peking, my attention has been drawn to reports from press agencies which allege that some members of the Ghana armed forces supported by some members of the police have attempted to overthrow my government—the government of the Convention People's Party.
>
> I know that the Ghanaian people are always loyal to me, the Party and the Government, and all I expect of everyone at this hour of trial is to remain calm, but firm in determination and resistance.
>
> Officers and men in the Ghana armed forces who are

involved in this attempt, are ordered to return to their barracks and wait for my return.

I am the constitutional head of the Republic of Ghana, and the supreme commander of the armed forces.

I am returning to Ghana soon."

I followed this up with a cable to all Ghanaian embassies:

"Be calm and remain firm at your posts. Send all messages and reports to me through the Ghana Embassy, Peking, and not, repeat not, through Accra until further notice."

As I discussed the news from Ghana with the 22 officials accompanying me, among them A. Quaison Sackey (Foreign Minister), Kwesi Armah (Minister of Trade), M. F. Dei-Anang (Ambassador Extraordinary, in charge of the African Affairs Secretariat), J. E. Bossman (Ambassador to the U.K.), F. Arkhurst (Ghana's Permanent Representative at the United Nations), I was somewhat disappointed to note their reaction. At a time like this, I would have expected them to show courage and fortitude. But most of them were frightened. Quaison Sackey, for example, developed diarrhoea, and must have visited the lavatory about twenty times that day. Their obvious dismay was in striking contrast to the calmness and courage of the 66 other personnel—the security officers and members of my personal secretariat. These were *men*. Compared with them, the politicians were old women.

With Alex Quaison Sackey, I will deal later. Kwesi Armah settled down in London where it appeared that he had considerable funds of money available to him. The rebel regime, on the basis of this, attempted to have him extradited on the grounds that he had stolen the money in question. His many trials before the English Courts exposed at least the falsity of the allegations which these authorities had made. I am glad that he was acquitted since I am sure that the particular charges made against him were false. Nonetheless, I believe that he brought his misfortunes on himself by failing to take a positive political stand. His various court cases however prove the nonsense contained in many of the allegations of corruption against my government.

Enoch Okoh and Michael Dei-Anang were old British

trained civil servants. They had made their way up through the colonial structure. They had been among my most trusted officials but they chose to return to Ghana, presumably in the hope that they would be accepted by the counter-revolutionaries.

Enoch Okoh, as head of the civil service and as the person who knew therefore which promotions had been made and why, was treated with leniency and was appointed to be in charge of the Housing Corporation. Since the new regime did not intend to build any houses for the people this was perhaps the appropriate punishment for his desertion.

Michael Dei-Anang was not so treated and, much to his surprise, was thrown into prison.

Fred Arkhurst, after his treachery, returned to his former position at the United Nations but was eventually removed by the 'N.L.C.' who could not trust someone who had, at least, ability.

Naturally, we were all of us anxious about the safety of our families in Ghana, but I suppose the official members of the party were also thinking about their bank accounts and their property. It is said that a man's heart lies where his treasure is. But even allowing for the fact that they had more to lose than the other personnel, I still find it hard to understand how they could have lost grip of themselves so easily. It was as though they had put their hands up at the first whiff of danger.

However, they did manage to pull themselves together sufficiently for me to be able to discuss the next moves with them. It was not until later, after they had left Peking, and were on their own, that the full depth of their defeatism became apparent, and they deserted.

We agreed that for the next day or two, while arrangements were being made, I should carry out official engagements as planned.

This was also the wish of the Chinese government. The Chinese made it clear that they regarded the military and police action in Ghana as no more than a temporary obstacle in the long struggle against imperialism, the kind of event to be expected, but which had no effect whatsoever on the final outcome. "You are a young man," Chou En-lai told me, "you have another forty years ahead of you!"

At the banquet held in my honour on 24th February, Liu

12

Shao-chi spoke of Afro-Asian solidarity, and the African peoples' revolutionary struggle:

"Most of the African countries have won independence, but the African peoples' revolutionary struggle against imperialism is by no means completed. They still have to carry on this struggle in greater depth. The imperialists headed by the United States are more active than ever in pressing forward with their policies of neo-colonialism in an attempt to subvert independent African countries and suppress the anti-imperialist revolutionary struggle of the African peoples. In his latest book, 'Neo-Colonialism—The Last Stage of Imperialism', President Nkrumah gave a detailed description of neo-colonialism and explicitly pointed out that 'foremost among the neo-colonialists' is the United States, which is 'the very citadel of neo-colonialism'. However hard the imperialists may whip up revolutionary adverse currents, the anti-imperialist revolutionary struggles of the African peoples can never be suppressed but are bound to win final victory. The Chinese people have unswervingly stood on the side of the African peoples and resolutely support their just struggles."

He went on to condemn U.S. policy in Vietnam, and to expose the hypocrisy of American so-called peace moves. No direct mention was made of the news from Ghana, or the possibility that I might not proceed to Hanoi.

In my reply, I also attacked neo-colonialism, and said that final victory would rest with the common man. I went on to condemn U.S. aggression in Vietnam, and called for the complete withdrawal of all American forces from Vietnam so that peace negotiations could begin.

I knew that I could not now go to Hanoi. My duty lay first with the people of Ghana, and I was determined to return to Africa as quickly as possible. But I was sorry to have to abandon my mission as it was the second time that President Ho Chi Minh had asked me to go, and I wanted to do anything I could to help end the war. I was, and as far as I know, still remain the only head of state or government that the President of North Vietnam has invited to Hanoi to discuss

13

the war since the American phase began. When I informed him of my decision, he replied that I would be welcome in Hanoi at any future date.

During the next two days, while I continued to carry out official engagements and to deal with the messages which began to pour in from abroad, the Chinese could not have shown greater care for my safety. If anyone near to me so much as put his hand in his pocket he was instantly pounced upon by security officers. They trusted no one, not even the Ghanaians who were with me.

Messages of encouragement and support continued to arrive from heads of state and governments all over the world. Many African leaders offered me immediate hospitality. Among them were President Sékou Touré of Guinea, President Nasser of Egypt, President Nyerere of Tanzania and President Modibo Keita of Mali. I was very touched that they should declare their solidarity so quickly and with such generosity, and it was only after deep thought that I decided to accept the invitation of President Sékou Touré and the Political Bureau of the Guinean Democratic Party. I sent the following note to President Sékou Touré:

PEKING.
25th February 1966.

My dear Brother and President,

I have been deeply touched by your message of solidarity and support I have received today. It is true, as you say, that this incident in Ghana is a plot by the imperialists, neo-colonialists and their agents in Africa. As these imperialist forces grow more militant and insidious, using traitors to the African cause against the freedom and independence of our people, we must strengthen our resolution and fight for the dignity of our people to the last man, and for the unity of Africa. It is heartening to know that in this struggle we can count on the support and understanding of Africa's well-tried leaders like yourself.

I know that our cause will triumph and that we can look forward to the day when Africa shall be really united and free from foreign interference and the intrigues of saboteurs and puppets.

I am safe and well here in Peking, and I have sent my

special emissary who will deliver this message to you to let you know the plans I am making for my early return to Africa. I trust that you will give him every possible assistance for the fulfilment of his mission.

I shall visit you in Guinea soon.

With sincere and brotherly affection,

Shortly afterwards, I received a further message from President Sékou Touré:

The Political Bureau and the Government after a thorough analysis of the African situation following the seizure of power by the instruments of imperialism have decided:

1. To organise a national day of solidarity with the Ghanaian people next Sunday. Throughout the length and breadth of the country there will take place popular demonstrations on the theme of anti-imperialism.
2. To call on all progressive African countries to hold a special conference and take all adequate measures.

We think that the time factor is vital here, since it is important to make a riposte without further delay, by every means. Your immediate presence would be very opportune, it seems to us, and we are therefore impatiently waiting for you.

Yours very fraternally,
Ahmed Sékou Touré.

I do not propose to publish in full all the messages I received from Heads of State and governments. But I would like to quote from the messages of two other African leaders. First, the note from President Modibo Keita of Mali:

I am happy to hear that you are well. Please thank our comrades of the People's Republic of China for this important contribution to Africa's struggle for liberty and progress.

Yesterday, the 24th of February, we learned of the serious events which took place in Ghana and which do no credit to those who have provoked them.

For us, the authors of the coup d'état have committed an act of high treason . . . . This is one phase of the unremitting struggle waged by neo-colonialists and

15

imperialists against Africa which wishes to live in freedom and dignity and in friendship with all peoples who are peace-loving and who wish to build a just society. All Africans, conscious of the grave dangers posed to our peoples and our continent, should mobilise themselves to bar the way to neo-colonialism and imperialism.

The Malian people consider themselves engaged in this struggle.

Secondly, I quote from the message from Albert Margai then Prime Minister of Sierra Leone:

Whilst we are conscious of the many and divers forces working in Africa which daily and constantly strive to foil our struggle for the final emancipation of those still subject to colonial rule and our ultimate claims to unity, I have nevertheless formed great hope and fortitude in the courage of your convictions and determined efforts to defy all odds in refusing to accept the results of the recent revolt as a fait accompli. Please accept, my dear Brother, the assurance of my highest consideration, esteem and prayers for your personal well-being and safety.

Apart from the fact that Guinea and Ghana formed a union in 1961, and a strong bond of friendship exists between President Sékou Touré, the Political Bureau of the Guinea Democratic Party, the people of Guinea and myself, I wanted to go to a country as near to Ghana as possible.

This would leave no one in any doubt about my intention to take up the neo-colonialist challenge and to restore legal government in Ghana. Guinea is only some 300 miles from Ghana. Jet flying time between the two countries is a mere 30-40 minutes. From Guinea I knew I would be in a good position to carry on the African revolutionary struggle. I decided that we should all, with the exception of Quaison Sackey and Bossman, go to Guinea via Moscow.

Quaison Sackey as foreign minister was entrusted with a very important mission. He was to go to Addis Ababa to represent the legal government of Ghana at the O.A.U. conference of foreign ministers due to open there within a few days. Instead of rising to the occasion, and accepting this great chal-

16

lenge and responsibility, he went to Accra and offered his services to the neo-colonialist puppets, the so-called National Liberation Council. The latter, it seems, made little use of him. Traitors have no friends.

I heard of his betrayal when I arrived in Moscow on the first of March, and it was there that I was also told of Bossman's defection. By then, Kwesi Armah and other officials had left Moscow to deal, as they said, with "urgent private matters." They were to return to Moscow, and we were all to travel together to Conakry. Instead, they defected. I then decided to proceed at once to Guinea with my personal entourage and members of my Guard Department. I wanted no one with me who was faint-hearted or two-faced. Every member of my party knew he was free to leave at any time. The security officers and other members of my personal staff decided to remain with me.

The Russian government sent an aircraft to Peking to fetch me, and I left from an air-strip near Peking on 28th February. Before leaving, I made the following statement to the press:

> I think you all know that certain members of my armed forces have attempted to usurp political power in Ghana while I was on the way to Hanoi. What they have done, in fact, is to commit an act of rebellion against the Government of the Republic. I am determined to crush it without delay, and to do this I rely upon the support of the Ghanaian people and of Ghana's friends in the world.
>
> By the arrest, detention and assassination of ministers, the Party's civil servants, and trade unionists, and by the massacre of defenceless men and women, the authors of these insane acts of robbery, violence and anarchy have added brutality to their treason.
>
> Never in the history of our new Ghana have citizens, men and women been assassinated in cold blood. Never have their children become orphans for political reasons. Never before have Ghanaians, our people, been shot because of their political convictions.
>
> This is a tragedy of monstrous proportions. The excessive personal ambition and the insane acts of these military adventurers, if not stifled now, will not only

destroy the political, economic and social achievements of the last few years, but will also obstruct the course of the African revolution.

All that has been achieved by the Ghanaian people with the assistance of all our friends is in jeopardy.

I am returning to Ghana; I know that the friendly nations and people of good will everywhere will support me in restoring the constitutional government of Ghana.

I take this opportunity to express my sincere condolences to all the families whose valiant sons and daughters have given their lives in the defence of Ghana.

At this moment, as I leave Peking, the capital city of the People's Republic of China, I express my profound gratitude to the Chinese people and to their leaders for their support and their kind hospitality.

We landed near Moscow at dawn on 1st March, after a brief stop at Irkutsk in Siberia, and were met by leading Soviet government officials. After a busy day of talks I re-embarked at midnight for the flight to Guinea.

We touched down briefly in Yugoslavia, and in Algeria, and reached Conakry in the afternoon of Wednesday, 2nd March. It was wonderful to be on African soil again. Guinea was agog with excitement. President Sékou Touré and members of the Political Bureau of the Democratic Party were among the huge crowd at the airport to welcome me. A twenty-one gun salute was fired.

At a mass rally in the packed sports stadium in Conakry the following day, President Sékou Touré announced that I had been made Secretary-General of the Guinean Democratic Party and Head of State of Guinea. "The Ghanaian traitors," he said "have been mistaken in thinking that Nkrumah is simply a Ghanaian . . . . He is a universal man." It looked as though the entire population of Conakry was in the stadium that afternoon and I shall never forget the reception they gave to Sékou Touré and myself as we were driven round the arena in an open car. The crowds rose to their feet, cheering, shouting anti-imperialist and anti-neo-colonialist slogans, and waving placards: "Long live the African Revolution," "Long live

Kwame Nkrumah," "Long live Sékou Touré," "Down with neo-colonialists," etc. It was a deeply moving experience, and I found my thoughts turning to similar mass rallies held in the Polo Ground, Accra. The people of Ghana were now being made to suffer for something which was not of their own making. They had been overcome by powerful external forces, and by the plotting and deception of a few selfish and ambitious reactionaries.

President Sékou Touré made a long speech. I did not know at the time exactly what he said. He spoke in French, and my knowledge of that language was then sketchy. I understood that I had been presented to the people of Guinea, but had no idea that I had been made President. It was not until after the ceremony, when I heard the press reports, that the full realisation of my new appointment became clear to me.

Such a gesture of political solidarity must surely be without historical precedent. When our historians come to record the events of 1966 they will doubtless consider the action of the Guinean Government as a great landmark in the practical expression of Pan-Africanism.

In this way began one of the most fruitful and happiest periods of my life—the time I spent in Conakry, about which I shall write later in this book.

2

24th FEBRUARY 1966

One of the first things I did after my arrival in Guinea was to establish an efficient communications system so that I could be kept fully informed of what was happening inside Ghana. Almost at once I began to receive detailed eye-witness accounts of what actually took place on 24th February and in the dark days which followed the army and police usurpation of power. At the same time there began a steady flow of Ghanaians to visit me in Conakry, to tell me about what had happened in Ghana and to express their loyalty. Some of them had walked all the way; others had found quicker means of travel. But all came at great personal risk to themselves and their families. Letters also began to pour in, and gradually the full, terrible story of violence and bloodshed took shape, and has since been confirmed to me over and over again by innumerable people who were there at the time of the military and police action and saw what took place. Several of the eye-witnesses who came to me still bore the marks of the brutal attacks made on them.

The true account of the seizure of power in Ghana by traitors and neo-colonialists does not make pleasant reading. But the facts must be faced and put on record so that the enormity of the crime committed against the people of Ghana can be accurately assessed.

I left Accra on 21st February 1966. I was seen off at the airport by most of the leading government and Party officials, and by service chiefs. I recall the handshakes and the expressions of good wishes from Harlley, Deku, Yakubu, and others. These men, smiling and ingratiating, had all the time treason and treachery in their minds. They had even planned my assassination on that day, though they later abandoned the idea. I remember shaking hands with Major-General Barwah—to be murdered in cold blood three days later when he refused to surrender to the rebel army soldiers. I little thought then that I would never see him again, or that Zanerigu, Commander of the Presidential Guard Regiment, Kojo Botsio, Kofi Baako and other ministers who were there at the airport, would be shortly seized by renegade soldiers and policemen and thrown into prison.

After a week of so-called "manoeuvres," the operation began early in the morning of Wednesday, 23rd February 1966 when the garrison at Kumasi, numbering 600 men, was ordered to move southwards to Accra. On the way, the convoy of some 35 vehicles was met and halted by the two arch-traitors Colonel Emmanuel Kwesi Kotoka, Commander of the Second Infantry Brigade Group, and Major Akwasi Amankwa Afrifa of the Second Brigade. Kotoka had only recently been put in charge of the Kumasi garrison, and I had not yet confirmed his appointment.

Afrifa was left in command while Kotoka went to Accra to report progress to Commissioner of Police, John Willie Kofi Harlley and to find some soldier better known than himself to be the nominal head of the revolt. The man chosen was Major-General Ankrah even though the conspirators had thought so little of his abilities than they had not previously troubled to consult him. He was, however, one of the few officers who had held even the rank of major in colonial days and had seen service in the world war if only as a quartermaster. In the Congo he had shown some bravery and, at least, routine ability and I had decorated him for his services but essentially he was of mediocre calibre. He held the post of second in command in the armed forces after independence through seniority, not ability. He would not have been appointed even to this post but for the death shortly before of another senior officer. In 1965 I retired him. Undoubtedly, it was his lack of understanding of what was going on around him which recommended him as a figure-head to those manipulating the 'coup'.

The troops were then told that I intended sending them to fight in Vietnam and in Rhodesia, and that I had deserted Ghana taking with me £8 million. There was, they were told, no government left in Ghana, and it was their duty to assume control of the country to maintain law and order. Already, it was said, Russian planes were landing on a secret airstrip in northern Ghana. Furthermore a secret tunnel had been made from Flagstaff House, the presidential residence, to Accra airport, and for days Russians had been arriving. The only way to save Ghana, and to avoid being sent to fight in Vietnam, the troops were told, was to take Flagstaff House.

Several days after the military seizure of power, Kotoka and Afrifa appeared on Ghana TV congratulating themselves on their easy success. One remark stood out unmistakable and clear: "And you know, we didn't find any Russians at all— not one! Nor could we find any trace of that tunnel." This was followed by peals of laughter at the poor soldiers who had believed their story.

The first object of the military operation was to force the surrender of Major-General Barwah, Army Chief of Staff and Deputy Chief of Defence Staff, who was in command of the Ghana Army in the absence from the country of the Chief of Defence Staff, General Aferi. At the same time, Brigadier Hasan, Head of Military Intelligence, and Colonel Zanerigu, Commander of the Presidential Guard Regiment, and Owusu-Sekyere, former head of the C.I.D. and in charge of the Special Branch, were to be arrested.

This stage of the operation was badly bungled. Hasan was arrested, but Zanerigu, when confronted, escaped through a window of his house and drove to Flagstaff House to warn the Presidential Guard Regiment. Barwah could not be intimidated. Woken from his sleep in the early hours of the morning of the 24th by the arrival of Kotoka and some 25 men, he courageously refused either to join the traitors or to surrender. Thereupon, Kotoka shot him dead at point-black range in cold blood in the presence of his wife and children. The seven security officers who were stationed at Barwah's house were also murdered on the spot on Kotoka's orders.

Kotoka subsequently boasted of his killing of Barwah but said because he was protected by a "juju" he was able to catch the bullets which Barwah fired in his defence and to throw them back at him. When the counter coup of April 1967 took place Kotoka's "magic" could not save him. Unlike Barwah he surrendered without protest or struggle to those who had captured him at his headquarters. His "juju" did not prevent him being shot in his turn.

Barwah's murder was one of the most disgraceful and ghastly crimes ever committed in Ghana's history. In an attempt to wipe the blood from their hands the so-called "N.L.C." gave Barwah and the security officers a military burial a few days later. What a mockery, and what hypocrisy! Yet these terrible, cold-blooded murders were only the first of many which occurred on 24th February and during subsequent days. They set the tone, as it were, of the whole operation which was characterised throughout by cowardice, bloodshed and criminal stupidity.

By 6 a.m. on the 24th, the Accra police, acting on Harlley's orders, had rounded up most of the ministers and other key political figures, and fighting had broken out at Flagstaff House between members of the Presidential Guard Regiment and rebel army units. There were about thirty members of the Guard Regiment at Flagstaff House when the alarm was raised. These were soon joined by others who managed to slip in by a back entrance to reinforce their comrades. Although heavily outnumbered they successfully held up the rebel detachment sent to seize the Ghana radio station a short distance from Flagstaff House. Only eight of the 124 detailed for this operation managed to get through. These captured the radio station, apparently without incident, and at 6 a.m. Kotoka arrived to broadcast that the army and police had taken over the government of Ghana.

The announcement was premature. At 7 a.m. resistance was actually increasing at Flagstaff House, as the defenders, less than a hundred of them, fought fiercely back against some 600 rebel troops. By this time a battalion in Accra under Ocran had joined them, not knowing what the fighting was all about. Thus the rebels were able to gain control of the airport, cable office, radio station, and all the approach roads to Accra.

Kotoka had established a combined H.Q. with the police at Police Headquarters, and from there the order was given for the 2nd Battalion to go into action at Flagstaff House. The Guard Regiment fought on, though their position was now hopeless. The outside walls of Flagstaff House had been blasted open, and the defenders had retreated behind the second gate. Still they refused to surrender. It was only after the rebels threatened to blow up the family residence at Flagstaff House in which my wife and three young children were sheltering that they finally gave in.

The fierce fighting at Flagstaff House at this time was in striking contrast to the failure at the time of the April 1967 counter-coup of Kotoka's body guard to defend his head-quarters. He had made Flagstaff House into a strong point from which he commanded the army. Yet when it was attacked by a small detachment of some 25 men the garrison immediately surrendered as did that of the Broadcasting Station which was also only attacked by a force of similar size. Again a small group of soldiers, not more than 50 in all, were sufficient to capture the Castle at Osu from which the "N.L.C." conducted their government. Ankrah 'the Chairman' of the "N.L.C." was the first of its defenders to run away, jumping over the Castle wall, plunging into the sea and wading down the shore.

What followed the fall of Flagstaff House on 24th February 1966, has been concealed from the world. But the people of Ghana know, and will never forget.

It may be explained in part by the fact that the soldiers who had carried out the 'coup' were frightened men. They had been told that there was a great store of arms beneath Flagstaff House and a hidden Russian army was concealed there which would suddenly emerge to attack them. They were jittery and fired on anyone on the slightest suspicion. They so frightened officials of the Japanese Embassy that they put placards on all their cars saying "We are NOT Chinese". There was also potential indiscipline. Despite the fact that Ghanaian armed forces in the Congo were regarded as the best of the African troops stationed there, the habit of drug-taking and excessive drinking which some of the soldiers had acquired there led to a mutiny in one battalion in which the Commanding Officer was so badly injured that he was left for dead, and in which the mutinous soldiers took over for two or three days complete control of the camp. In order to restore discipline it had been necessary to disband this battalion.

The officers who organised the "coup", having deceived their men, were now in no position to discipline them.

Rebel troops, many of them almost mad from the effects of Indian hemp which had been issued to them, others intoxicated with alcohol looted from ransacked houses and trigger-happy,

24

carried out the most cruel and senseless attacks on innocent men, women and children. Thousands of pounds worth of damage was done to government property, and valuable historical documents and records were destroyed.

At Flagstaff House itself, troops dashed from one room to another, smashing windows and furniture, tearing up papers, ripping telephones from desks, and destroying anything they could lay their hands on. My own office was singled out for special treatment. The full extent of the loss of books and manuscripts I shall discover on my return. I am hoping that by some miracle the precious notes I was compiling for a history of Africa may have been spared. If not, years of work will have been wasted, and the labour of collecting and sorting material and writing it up will have to begin again from scratch.

The stupidity of this needless destruction of government property, and the failure of the rebel officers to exercise any control over their men, demonstrates the quality of their leadership.

In the six-roomed two-storey house where I lived with my family, troops were allowed to run riot, seizing clothes and other intimate personal possessions including rare old books and manuscripts. My wife and children, although not physically harmed, were not permitted to take a single thing with them when they were turned out of the house and forced to take refuge in the Egyptian Embassy.

My mother, 80 years old and almost blind, who was staying at Flagstaff House, was forcibly ejected and told to go "where you belong". I understand some friends took her to Nkroful where I was born. Later, the actual house in which I was born was burnt down on "N.L.C." orders.

My mother was forced to appear before a 'commission of enquiry' with the idea of making her admit that I was not her son and indeed was not a Ghanaian at all. I am proud to know that she resolutely refused to say anything of the sort and conducted herself with the utmost dignity.

From Flagstaff House, the troops went to Kanda Estate where many security officers have their quarters. There they hurled grenades into the compounds, broke into houses and flats, tossed furniture out of the windows, and carried off radios, refrigerators and other property. Anyone who resisted them was brutally shot. Women, children and old people were driven out into the streets. Many of the women were raped. Even young children were hit with rifle butts. A woman with a child on her back was shot, and both mother and child were thrown to the ground from a three-storey window.

The rank and file police who had taken no part in the 'coup' were horrified at what was taking place and did their best to restrain the soldiers and this led in some cases to actual fighting between the two forces.

Meanwhile, the soldiers had been reinforced by a new element. It was part of the propaganda against Ghana abroad and internally that my government had detained thousands of individuals. There were, of course, political detainees but their number, for state security, was fortunately small. Most of these detainees under the Preventive Detention Act were the so-called "criminal" detainees. As industrialisation developed in Ghana so, as in all countries, organised crime increased and at one stage in the immediate post-independence period we were faced with a situation which, if we had not dealt with it, would have resulted in the country being terrorised by organised criminal gangs. The view of the police was that it was not possible in many cases, any more than it was in the United States at some periods of its history, to secure convictions in courts of the gang leaders or of their supporters. The Preventive Detention Act was therefore extended to cover habitual criminals suspected of gangsterism.

If the rebels had only released the genuine political detainees the total would have been so small as to discredit them and in any case they required the prison accommodation occupied by the criminal detainees in order to lock up anyone suspected of being a C.P.P. member or supporter. In the days following the 'coup' the criminal detainees were not only released but were able to represent themselves as "the heroes of the counter-revolution". By day they joined, naturally, in the demonstrations against my government and at night returned to their old activities to such an extent that even the strictly controlled "N.L.C." press demanded that they should be returned to prison.

Accra was handed over to lawless elements which the rank and file police had no means of controlling. Bar owners were forced at gun point to sell free beer to soldiers and to the "heroes of the counter-revolution", the criminal detainees. These people assaulted women, thieved, and looted. It will be only after the return to legal government in Ghana that it will be possible to assess exactly the number of those who died in fighting against the rebel soldiers or were subsequently killed in the looting and robbery which followed. The casualties in the fighting were certainly heavy. The number of civilians killed, it is more difficult to estimate. Two members of Parliament certainly lost their lives and a number of people in no way connected with politics died. Among those shot dead near Flagstaff House was an air hostess on her way to the airport. In all, the total was probably around 1,600 dead and many more injured. So much for the "bloodless coup"!

One thing is clear. Never before in the cherished history of our new Ghana had citizens, defenceless men and women, been assassinated in cold blood by their own soldiers. Not a single Ghanaian life was taken during the whole fifteen years of my administration. There are few, if any, governments in the world which can say as much. Yet here was this handful of traitors at one blow spoiling our proud record, and dragging Ghana's name through the mud.

In the days which followed the insurrection, hundreds of patriotic Ghanaians were thrown into prison. All ministers, M.P.s, officials of the Party and of all its subsidiary and associate organisations including the trade unions were arrested and detained. The same applied to branch officers throughout the country. In fact, the entire leadership, except for the few who managed to escape or go into hiding, was at one swoop rounded up and thrown into prison.

The prison authorities, with some exceptions, continued to act in the humane and considerate way which we had insisted upon in the prison service, since the establishment of independence. The Director of Prisons, in particular, saw to it that no one, insofar as he could prevent it, once inside the prison, was ill-treated. It is significant that subsequently he was pronounced by the "N.L.C." to have become insane and taken to a lunatic asylum where he died, mysteriously electrocuted.

Professor Kojo Abraham, Fellow of All Souls, Oxford, and a former Governor of the School of Oriental and African Studies in London, was mercilessly beaten when soldiers

27

arrived to arrest him. He was flung unconscious into the police van. Abraham, at the time of his arrest, was an M.P. and Acting Vice-Chancellor of the University of Ghana. His only crime was that he was a leading member of the Party. The manuscript of a new book he was writing was among the first of a pile of papers and books publicly burnt, Nazi-style, by the mutinous soldiers who arrested him.

Geoffrey Bing, Q.C., a distinguished British lawyer, and one of my legal advisers, who had come to Ghana at Government invitation to help in our legal and constitutional work, had his clothes and shoes torn off him and was made to walk up and down barefoot and to stand up and sit down in repeated succession without being able to use his hands. Bayonets were stuck into his back, and it was not until a Commander of the Ghana Navy arrived on the scene that they stopped torturing him.

Typical of the sort of thing which happened was the wounding of the Deputy Manager of one of the hotels in Accra. He was being driven by his driver on hotel business but suddenly was shot by a soldier. The explanation subsequently given was that as he was sitting at the back of the car the soldier thought he must have been a minister in my government.

These are only a few examples of the countless acts of brutality carried out within the first week or so, by the traitorous renegades and cowards who seized power in Ghana on 24th February 1966. The people of Ghana were stunned. Nobody outside Accra knew what had happened, or was happening. In some cases, particularly in the remoter districts, it was days before they realised what had taken place. Even then, the full implications of the army and police action dawned only slowly as they began gradually to see through the lies poured out over the radio and in the press, and saw with their own eyes the way in which the independence and progress of their beloved country was being destroyed, and its assets sold to foreign interests.

In Accra, military police and soldiers in full battle dress and armed with sub-machine guns patrolled the streets. In such circumstances, and with all the Party leadership arrested, it was not surprising that there was no immediate and open resistance. But secret, underground resistance began at once.

28

It grew by leaps and bounds.

While a number of the ministers hastened to ingratiate themselves with the rebels, others remained firm. Nothing for example has been heard of N. A. Welbeck, Minister of Information and Party Propaganda who resolutely refused to make any cringing retraction of his past political activities. And the same is true of other ministers such as I. K. Chinebuah, Minister of Education and former Headmaster of Achimota School. The most heartening demonstration, however, came from the resolute attitude adopted by many of those in the intermediate and lower ranks of the Party.

The journalists, regional commissioners, district commissioners and party secretaries were imprisoned in the central block of Ussher Fort prison. Almost from the first day of their imprisonment onward they were singing in chorus Party songs so loudly that they could be heard well outside the prison and this despite the fact that their block was patrolled by armed soldiers.

Ghanaians are not a timid people as has been suggested in the foreign press. Far from it. They may be slow to anger, and may take time to organise and act. But once they are ready they strike, and strike hard. It pays no one to tamper with Ghanaian freedom and dignity. Ghana is out of the gambling house of colonialism, and will never return to it.

The American, British and European press has made much of the "demonstrations" which occurred in Accra in celebration of the 'coup'. It is interesting, however, that even in the Ghanaian papers there were no reports of any such demonstrations in the villages or in the country-side where one would have expected them, if the revolt had been genuinely popular. It is understandable however that certain elements, particularly in Accra, should demonstrate in favour of the new regime. The criminal detainees naturally led the celebrations but they were joined by more sober citizens. The intellectuals and the professional classes had always been against my government which they felt, quite rightly, was challenging their position of privilege. The lawyer and the clergyman thus found themselves joining in the same processions through the streets as the criminal. There was a section of the market women who had been exploiting the shortage of goods due to the measures which we had to take for the control of non-essential imports. They had been exposed by the Abraham Commission and they naturally were delighted that its Chairman should have now been thrown into jail. In addition to this there were at the start a number of people who were genuinely deceived by the revolt.

The disastrous fall in the world price of cocoa had led to inevitable import shortages of consumer goods. These people really believed that the 'coup' would change all this, and so they joined the gangs in the streets. Others joined them out of curiosity. Even so it was necessary for the army to force children from their school rooms and to dragoon demonstrators in order to make a satisfactory show. A small number of students from the university at Legon, wanting to demonstrate in favour of the new regime, asked for and were given police protection, so fearful were they of the reaction of the people of Accra. It was not until instructions were issued from police headquarters that the first street "demonstrations" took place.

Banners and posters, most of them prepared beforehand in the U.S. Embassy, were pushed into the hands of the unwilling "demonstrators". Many of the slogans and words used on them were quite foreign to the Ghanaian people, and in some cases completely incomprehensible. The same kind of thing was noticeable in the newspapers and news bulletins issued immediately after the seizure of power. Words and phrases were used which had never been seen in a Ghanaian newspaper before. The same discrepancy occurred on the radio as bulletins and news flashes were broadcast. The voice was Ghanaian, but the unfamiliar words and the glib expressions were foreign, and often caused the announcer to hesitate and falter.

Clearly, the polished editorials, news bulletins and unfamiliar slogans had been devised by experts trained in the art of overthrowing "undesirable governments", but who had not taken the trouble to familiarise themselves with the Ghanaian way of thinking or expression.

I understand that the Uganda government in its investigations following the abortive coup which took place in Kampala on 26th February, only two days after the action in Accra, discovered prepared news bulletins, posters and newspaper editorials which were strikingly similar in style and content to those actually used in Ghana. I leave the reader to draw the obvious conclusions.

In the Makola market, a woman who had a large picture of myself above her stall was shot dead by an army officer after refusing three times to hand it over for destruction. This kind of incident, not seen by foreign journalists, who obediently and very willingly photographed and reported only the staged demonstrations and rigged press interviews, was typical of many other pathetic but deeply moving acts of heroism performed by the ordinary men and women of Ghana during those dark days.

Much publicity was given in the imperialist press and on T.V., to the pulling down of the statue of myself in front of the National Assembly building in Accra. It was made to appear as though angry crowds had torn the statue from its pedestal and had carried off chunks of it. But it was not for nothing that no photographs could be produced to show the actual pulling down of the statue; and the few women seen carrying away portions of the statue on their heads were photographed backview. In fact when the statue was pulled down the Parliament building where it stood had been cordoned off by the military and no unauthorised person was allowed into the area. All those who were there at the time had been those brought in by the military, who had closed to all civilians the whole of the High Street onto which the statue faced. When the statue had been pulled down about half-a-dozen terrified young children were forced to sit on it as it lay on the ground. Even the jubilant imperialist press evidently saw nothing strange in publishing photographs of bewildered toddlers, tears running down their cheeks, sitting on a headless statue, while the same imperialist press extolled what it described as a "most popular coup". Since even the women shown carrying away pieces of it on their heads were photographed from behind, it is impossible to be certain whether they were from a group of the market women condemned by the Abraham Commission or, as was widely rumoured in Accra, "soldiers dressed up as women".

There are many other incidents which could be recorded, but sufficient has been written to show the manner in which the military and police action of 24th February 1966 was carried out.

Of course there were some who were happy at the turn of events. In any country there are always elements glad to see a change of government, and the traitors among the army and police who seized power in my absence could not even have attained the degree of success they did manage to achieve without support. The nature of this support, internal and external, I now intend to examine.

3

THE "NATIONAL LIBERATION COUNCIL"

In a proclamation published on 26th February 1966 the people of Ghana were told that the constitution had been suspended and that a "National Liberation Council" had been established which constituted the new government of Ghana. According to this proclamation, I and all my ministers were dismissed from office, the National Assembly was dissolved, and the Convention People's Party disbanded. Further, the "N.L.C." assumed full powers to make and issue decrees "which shall have the force of law in Ghana" and to appoint committees to administer their "affairs of state".

The proclamation ended, as it had begun, with the names of the eight traitors who formed the "N.L.C.":

J. A. Ankrah, Chairman (Army)
J. W. K. Harlley, Deputy Chairman (Police)
E. K. Kotoka, Member (Army)
B. A. Yakubu, Member (Police)
A. K. Ocran, Member (Army)
J. E. Nunoo, Member (Police)
A. A. Afrifa, Member (Army)
A. K. Deku, Member (Police).

It was in this way that the people of Ghana were informed of the names of their so-called liberators. Few had ever heard of them. They were nonentities. Yet here they were, four soldiers and four policemen, arrogantly claiming, without any shred of a mandate from the people, that they constituted "the new government of Ghana". Small wonder Ghanaians were at first stunned, and then became increasingly incensed as this clique of misguided and ignorant upstarts proceeded to unmask not only themselves but their neo-colonialist masters. Very soon they became universally known not as the

"National Liberation Council" but as the Notorious Liars Council, a name I gave them when I spoke to the people of Ghana on Radio Guinea's Voice of the Revolution soon after my arrival in Conakry.

In a booklet entitled "The Rebirth of Ghana" the members of the "N.L.C." found it necessary to publish photographs of themselves, selected facts about their shoddy careers, and information about their shady characters and trivial hobbies. It reads rather like excerpts from a poor imitation of the well-known British directory of notable personalities: "Who's Who." We are told that Ankrah was born in 1915, was a "keen sportsman" at school, and was trained at the Officer Cadet Training Unit in Britain. We are informed that "he is companionable, friendly and full of good humour". The authors of the booklet, gluttons for unnecessary detail, go on to say that Ankrah's hobbies are "gardening, films and an occasional swim". Not a very fitting list of interests and hobbies for the Chairman of the so-called National Liberation Council. No mention, of course, is made in the booklet of the fact that I found it necessary to dismiss Ankrah in 1965. He was becoming lazy, incompetent and unreliable. In addition to this, Ankrah and Major-General Otu revealed to me that they had, on several occasions, been written to anonymously and asked to join plots to overthrow the government. It seemed to me that, even if they had refused to join, their names had become associated with treason, and they should no longer continue to serve in the Ghana army. I retired them, gave them six months' pay, gratuities, and positions in two of the leading Accra banks.

Harlley, we are told, was born in 1919 at Akagla in the Volta Region. He enlisted in the Ghana Police service in 1940 and rose through the ranks to become inspector in 1952. He then went to the Metropolitan Police College in Hendon, England, and on his return to Ghana was step by step promoted to become head of the Special Branch. I was amused to read that he is "of a quiet disposition, considerate, kind-hearted, but very firm". And it is edifying to learn that "he enjoys the sight and sound of water, but hates to see fire or anything connected with burning". Again, not very inspiring qualifications for political leadership. Harlley, we are finally told, is married and has eight children. This is evidently considered respectable.

We are not told about Ankrah's four wives and 22 children.

Kotoka, generally credited with commanding the actual military operations on 24th February, was also trained in Britain. In fact, all members of the "N.L.C." were trained in the U.K. The four policemen were at the Metropolitan Training College in Hendon and the four soldiers at various British army training centres, though only Afrifa, the youngest, managed to get to Sandhurst.

We are informed that Kotoka "is a fine soldier, disciplined, loyal, resolute and firm". I must confess I am unimpressed by his "discipline" and "loyalty".

When his name was flashed across the headlines of the world press on 24th February, I had hardly heard of him. At the time when I reorganised the armed forces, he came to Flagstaff House to take the oath of allegiance to me as Supreme Commander of the Ghana armed forces. Kotoka was the only one late in arriving. I remember turning to Aferi, Chief of Defence Staff at that time and asking: "Who is this chap?"

As for Ocran, for a time my A.D.C., he is described as "rather reserved; shy of publicity". His interests are simply "bird watching". Yakubu, after a "brilliant career in the Inspectorate", rose gradually to the rank of Deputy Commissioner of Police. He is the only Northerner on the "N.L.C.," and his inclusion was doubtless for political reasons. Yet, like his colleagues on the "N.L.C.", he makes no claim to either political interests or experience. He is "quiet and always smiling" and likes to do farm work in his spare time.

Little space is given to Nunoo. After a brief sketch of his police career we are informed that he "has a pleasant baritone voice, and has sung in choirs and choral societies for over 15 years." He might have been more suitably employed, one would think, on Ghana radio or television.

The last two members of the "N.L.C." to be written about, Afrifa and Deku, leave the reader finally in no doubt about the quality of Ghana's so-called "new government". Afrifa, born in 1936 was one of those typical mis-fits which are produced in any developing society. As a school boy he had been expelled from Adisadel school and therefore could not obtain the university education for which he was hoping. Instead he joined the army and exploited his School Certificate education so as to be sent to Sandhurst. Indeed he was the only one among the mutinous officers who had had the conventional British army training. As he himself confesses, even when he was a senior cadet at Sandhurst he was always doing punishment drills for insubordination. It was only because we were desperately short of officers to serve in the Congo that he was commissioned at all. The fact that he had served there led to his securing rapid promotion and at the time of the 'coup' he was a major.

Anthony Deku was a typical colonial policeman. In colonial days Michael Collins, the English Commissioner of Police, in the days before my arrest and imprisonment sued me for libel as publisher of the *Evening News* for what I had written about the conduct of the colonial police. He persuaded Deku to be his co-plaintiff so as to make his action appear not to be exclusively European versus African. It was part of what I think now may have been a mistaken policy of letting all by-gones be by-gones that I never allowed this fact to prejudice his subsequent promotion in the Police Service.

If it were not for the great harm these traitors have done to our beloved Ghana, we could laugh at them. They appear so ridiculous. None of them makes any claim to an interest in politics; and not one of them has any political experience. How could men such as these imagine for one moment that they had any hope of successfully administering the country? Their stupidity can only be matched by their conceit. But we cannot laugh when we see what suffering and destruction they have caused in their attempt to sabotage our great struggle for economic independence, and our efforts in the African Revolution to achieve the total liberation of the continent and a Union Government of Africa. Were it not for the support of a small reactionary element inside Ghana, and the help of neo-colonialists, they could not have organised and carried out the action of 24th February 1966, much less have maintained themselves in power for even a few months.

It is necessary to look more closely at the leadership of the army, police and civil service in order to understand how it became possible for these reactionary, counter-revolutionary forces, internal and external, to make use of them.

It has been said, particularly by well-wishers from outside

Ghana, that if I knew of the potential disloyalty in the army why did I not deal with it? The very posing of this question discloses the fundamental misunderstanding about the Ghanaian position as it existed before the 'coup' in many friendly circles abroad.

As I then saw it, my task was two-fold. On the one hand, I had to secure a firm basis in Ghana and on the other, conduct an external policy which would lead to the liberation and unity of the whole African continent, and to the economic co-operation which was essential if any territory in Africa was to escape from neo-colonialism. In the military sense these two aims were contradictory.

I could, for example, have avoided any risk of a military revolt by maintaining the system which the British Government assumed would be maintained after independence, by which Britain would continue to supply for 10 to 15 years our key military personnel. The individual loyalties of such officers and their training, combined with the political complications for Britain which would have resulted in their joining in a revolt, would have made it unlikely that a military take-over could take place. On the other hand, if I maintained a non-African officered army, Ghana could not play a significant military part in the affairs of the continent.

Yet the tragedy of the Congo made one thing absolutely clear, that even small African forces on the spot at the right time could control the situation and prevent a neo-colonialist take-over. I therefore was not in a position to abolish the Ghanaian army, though this would have been an ideal course. It was a heavy charge on our limited resources for industrial development. On the other hand, looking at the problem from a continental point of view, if Ghana had no armed forces at all it must lose much of its influence with other African states. I have always said that for me the issue of African unity came before any other consideration. It was for this reason that I was prepared to run the risk of maintaining for the time being a traditional British-type army.

A Ghanaian army with British officers could have no influence in Africa. In the first place, while British officers were prepared to be loyal to the regime they were serving they were not prepared, as General Alexander, the last British Commander of the Ghanaian army says very frankly in his memoirs, to follow a military policy abroad which was contrary to what they conceived to be Britain's interests. Secondly, even if the British officers had been pure mercenaries, with no allegiance other than to their paymasters, they would still have been rightly distrusted by other African states. Once therefore the Congo crisis arose, irrespective of any question of internal security, it became necessary to dispense with the British officers.

Unfortunately, the "preparations" for independence had not included the training of anything like sufficient officers or even NCO's to make it possible for me to choose on political grounds who should be promoted. There were, in fact, insufficient soldiers with the necessary training or qualifications to fill even half the positions left vacant by the departing British. In order to have an army at all, I therefore had to accept what existed even though I knew the danger of this course. In fact, the most efficient of the British trained Ghanaian potential officer class were the most neo-colonialist. One or two of these I might pass over on this ground, but in general, if I was to have an army at all, I had to accept the framework bequeathed to me and an officer corps which contained a high proportion of individuals who were either actively hostile to the C.P.P. and myself and who were anti-socialist in outlook. Worse still, the fact that the bulk of the infantry came from the North, where education had been almost completely neglected in colonial times, made many of the rank and file soldiers easy prey to anyone who wished to mislead them.

In regard to the police the problem was even more complex. We were going forward rapidly with the development of the economy and industrialisation. As experience throughout the world has shown, even the movement of population this must occasion breaks down old traditional restraints and a criminal class rapidly develops in expanding towns. By independence, crime had become a real problem in Ghana where many transactions such as cocoa buying are conducted in cash and where the import of quantities of constructional material and the like provides a ready market for the thief. Further and even more important, I was faced with the problem of financial corruption and a well organised Fraud Division in the Police was essential if this was to be held in check. I could not however possibly continue with the existing British police officers. Prior to 1951 Michael Collins, the British Commissioner of Police had not only brought various personal court cases against me arising out of my political activities but was so contemptuous of the change in the political atmosphere that, even after my release from prison and my appointment as Prime Minister, he continued to demand from me, and indeed received payment, for the balance of the damages awarded him by the colonial court. The rank and file police officers who were loyal to the C.P.P. would not have tolerated the retaining in command of such persons. On the other hand, it was impossible immediately to make promotions to the higher ranks of police, men who had had training in detective work or administration. As with the army, I therefore had to accept a police force many of whose higher officers were politically hostile to the new Ghana. They, after all, had been those chosen for promotion by the colonial regime and they had thus a monopoly of the specialist training required. Further many of them were corrupt but to obtain proof of this was a difficult matter.

I tried in these circumstances to build up a new security service which would be completely independent of the police force, but to obtain its personnel I had to go to the civil service and the conduct of Eric Otoo the Civil Servant I put in charge shows how unreliable was the support I could get from this quarter.

The third element supporting the present regime is, in fact, the civil service. Again, I was faced at independence with similar problems to those that I had with the army and the police. For example, it would be impolitic for me to have appointed abroad a former colonial British civil servant as a Ghanaian Ambassador. I had to appoint Ghanaians for the diplomatic service.

The Information Services which were the most important channel in letting the people know what was taking place and the reasons for any particular government action were all manned by civil servants originally trained by the old colonial Information Department which had been set up specifically to conduct propaganda against the C.P.P. and the idea of colonial independence .

However, I was able to pick and choose among the civil

service much more than I was with the army and the police and I was able, in many cases, to reform the diplomatic and the information services. Despite this, throughout the public service as a whole, there was a tradition of serving whatever government was in power. Many of the senior officials had all originally served with the old colonial regime which had opposed trade unionism and socialism in any form and was against any real representation of the people in government. After the C.C.P.'s victory in 1951 they changed over to administer the new ideas, becoming supporters of "enlightened colonialism".

When colonialism gave way to independence, these same men gave support to the new order of things. As gradually we changed social and political conditions in Ghana they accepted the changes without protest and though there may have been a degree of sabotage behind the scenes, always openly proffered their support for my policies and that of my Party.

In such circumstances it is only natural that they should have in the first place uncritically accepted the rebel government. Indeed behind the scenes the civil servants always looked back to the colonial times when their senior members were described as "political officers" and they in practice ran the country. They welcomed the military revolt because they believed that behind the facade of military power they would be the real rulers. It is only now that they are becoming disillusioned and are discovering that however incompetent in administration and politics senior military and police officers are, those who have seized power are determined to use their authority to maintain their own personal interests.

There is quite a record of police hostility towards me personally and towards my government. It dates back to pre-independence days when I was campaigning for freedom from colonial rule, and the British government founded the Special Branch in Ghana to keep an eye on me. For years, members of the Special Branch were trained to regard me as a dangerous man whose political views and activities threatened all that was stable and respectable in British eyes. Harlley, Deku and Nunoo all served in the Special Branch. Nunoo actually gave evidence against me in my trial after the declaration of Positive Action. Old habits die hard, and I regret now that I did not abolish the Special Branch in 1957, at independence. It was a typically British creation, and really had no place in our society. But it was thought at the time that it might prove useful in some areas of police work. In fact, members of the police and Special Branch have been involved in each of the six attacks made on my life, and have frequently ignored, and sometimes aided, the activities of people they knew were plotting to overthrow the government.

In 1958 the General Secretary of the Opposition Party, R. R. Amponsah, and one of its leading Members of Parliament, M. K. Apaloo, who was the Opposition spokesman on military matters, entered into a conspiracy with Major Benjamin Ahwaitey who was then the most senior of the Ghanaian officers and was Camp Commandant of Burma Camp. The plot leaked out and Amponsah was arrested at the beach where he had gone to meet Ahwaitey. A very full enquiry was held in public but undoubtedly the full facts and the extent to which the Opposition as a whole was involved did not come out.

In the enquiries conducted after the bomb attack on me at Kulungugu on 1st August 1962 in which several innocent people lost their lives, it was also discovered that leading police officers were closely involved. Before Obetsebi Lamptey, one of the ringleaders in the plot to kill me, was caught, Special Branch knew that he was going around dressed as a Moslem, and had even entered the Parliament building in Accra, yet they did not arrest him.

On a later occasion, on 1st January 1964, another attempt was made on my life. On this occasion it was a policeman who actually made the attempt. It was at 1 p.m. in the garden of Flagstaff House. I was leaving the office to go for lunch when four shots were fired at me by one of the policemen on guard duty. He was no marksman, though his fifth shot succeeded in killing Salifu Dagarti, a loyal security officer who had run towards the would-be assassin as soon as he spotted him among the trees. The policeman then rushed at me, trying to hit me with his rifle butt. I wrestled with him and managed to throw him to the ground and to hold him there on his back until help came, but not before he had bitten me on the cheek.

Investigation showed that the policeman who had made the attempt on my life did not happen to be in Flagstaff

House by accident. He had been picked by senior police officers one of whom had repeatedly invited him to his home. At around the same time came the revelation of another unsuccessful plot within the police. The officer in charge of the Police Band which used to play at official functions approached two friends of his among the bandsmen and suggested to them that they should shoot me with revolvers which he would provide when I came over as I always did to congratulate them on their performance. Fortunately the two men not only would have nothing to do with the plot but reported it, as did independently the policemen who had been approached to smuggle into Flagstaff House the weapons required. In such circumstances I considered it best to make a clean sweep of the top command in the police and Madjitey, the Commissioner of Police, and his Deputy, Amaning, were arrested together with the bandmaster. In view of the events of February 1966 it was a great pity that there was not a complete reorganisation of the police service from top to bottom. However, at the time it appeared not really practical to change the whole structure of the force without evidence that the next most senior officers had not been in any way involved in this or other conspiracies.

Thus it was that Harlley and Deku who had both served in the Special Branch came to be appointed Commissioner of Police and Head of the Criminal Investigation Department respectively. What I did not know then was that although they had exposed to me various criminal and corrupt acts of their colleagues, they themselves were involved in dubious dealings.

I had asked Geoffrey Bing who had been the Attorney-General to investigate racketeering in diamonds. It appeared that there was growing smuggling of Ghana diamonds and other malpractices in regard to their sale. After making enquiries, Bing came to suspect a European diamond dealer who had been made a prohibited immigrant in colonial times. This man had managed to return to Ghana but had been again deported. When Bing saw the Special Branch records he discovered that Harlley, using my name without my authority, had revoked the deportation order. I gave orders that the man should be arrested and deported again forthwith. When his private notebook was examined by the security services, it was found to contain the private home and office telephone numbers of Harlley and records of a conversation which he had had with Deku. Bing made a full report on this whole matter to Eric Otoo who however never forwarded it to me. I believe that one of the motives of Harlley and Deku in promoting the "coup" was that they feared exposure in this matter.

Certainly the "N.L.C." made the greatest efforts to secure Bing's arrest demanding him from the Australian High Commission where he had taken refuge. When he was in their custody he was continually interrogated as to what he knew about the diamond matter and was kept in prison for a month. His secretary, an English lady who had served continuously in Ghana from colonial days, was placed under house arrest and not allowed to leave until she had found and handed over personally to Deku all the papers in Bing's wrecked office which dealt with diamond smuggling. Bing's subsequent deportation was not an act of grace by the regime but an attempt to hush up the reason for his arrest.

It was Harlley and his close associates who subverted the army and persuaded certain officers to carry out the military side of the operation. Afrifa, in the apologia which appeared in his name in November 1966, boasts that he thought of a military "coup" as far back in 1961. Incidentally, I was amused to see that he used the final sentences from my Autobiography as the opening to the Postscript of his book, though he makes no acknowledgement, and the passage appears without quotation marks. Kotoka has also claimed credit for the "coup." In fact, immediately after the "N.L.C." was proclaimed there was a positive rush to claim entire credit for the betrayal of Ghana. In London, Daniel Amihia, calling himself the leader of the African Democratic Party, whatever that may be, appeared on B.B.C./T.V., resplendent in a new shantung suit and said that he had "master-minded the coup". He boasted that he had been trained by the U.S. Central Intelligence Agency (C.I.A.) and the Americans did not deny this. Amihia was lured back to Accra, publicly exposed as a "fraud" by the jealous "N.L.C.", and promptly thrown into prison and no one seems to know what has become of him. Kofi Busia, former opposition leader, was also interviewed by the B.B.C. in London. He was too much of a politician to say openly that he had plotted the overthrow of the constitutional government of Ghana, but obviously tried to give the impression that he had played an important part in planning the military and police action.

Doubtless, there were traitorous and disloyal thoughts in the minds of all those who carried out and supported the action of 24th February 1966. But I am convinced that it was Harlley and his close associates, inspired and aided by disgruntled former opposition party members and neo-colonialists, who were the real initiators. They alone possessed the necessary vital information needed for its success.

Much of this information they obtained from Eric Otoo, a civil servant whom I appointed chief executive officer in charge of security, and whom I left behind in Ghana in a position of great responsibility and trust when I departed for Hanoi. Otoo betrayed the trust put in him and revealed everything to the traitors. Without his co-operation they might not have succeeded. The moral wickedness of it astounds me. How a man trusted with such responsibility could assist a clique of traitors defies understanding.

For years traitors among the old colonial police had plotted the overthrow of my government. Their original idea was to kill. But having failed in several assassination attempts, and no doubt inspired by neo-colonialist aided military coups in other parts of Africa, they then decided to look for support in the army.

Police subversion of certain army officers was not difficult. Harlley knew and trusted Kotoka. They belonged to the same tribe (Ewe), both were born in the Volta Region, and even attended the same school. They met on many occasions in Kumasi and elsewhere and plotted. Kotoka then began to approach other officers, notably Afrifa, an Ashanti. There has always been a close link between the Ewes and Ashanti reactionary elements, and Kotoka judged rightly that Afrifa would be likely to respond favourably. So it went on, until a sufficient number of officers had been roped in.

Here I must make the point that only a relatively small number of officers were actually subverted. Once the rebellion had begun others offered no open resistance, for the majority were taken completely by surprise and were faced with a *fait accompli*.

44

The fact that Harlley and others found it fairly easy to get support in the army may also be explained by what has been called "the Sandhurst mentality" of certain officers. These men trained in various English military establishments prided themselves on being more "English" than Ghanaian, and tended to frown on everything in our Ghanaian way of life which did not conform with English customs and traditions. They gradually became more British than the British as they slavishly tried to imitate the traditional English army officer. Ankrah is a typical example with his enthusiasm for the Turf Club, his love of ceremonial, and his sense of caste.

Afrifa has called Sandhurst "one of the greatest institutions in the world". He looks with nostalgia on the days he spent there: "through its doors have passed famous generals, kings and rulers . . . It is an institution that teaches that all men are equal, that the profession of men-at-arms is essential and a peaceful one." The confusion in his mind is obvious.

Like many other army officers in the developing countries who have received part of their training in imperialist establishments, he had been brainwashed into showing more devotion to his counterparts in imperialist countries than to his own countrymen. He considered himself a "gentleman", far superior to the peasants and workers of his own country. He admits that it was while he was in Britain that he first heard criticism of the Ghanaian government. He listened to people running down our efforts to achieve economic independence. He read in the British press that I was a "dictator", and that Ghana had stepped out of line in establishing a one-party state and in pursuing such revolutionary aims as the complete liberation and unity of the African continent. Instead of being proud to be Ghanaian and in the vanguard of the African revolutionary struggle, he identified himself with the critics of his own government and people.

Afrifa's case history is similar to that of many more of our army officers in the independent states of Africa. While training in imperialist countries they became imbued with ideas and traditions which made them easy game for those plotting the overthrow of progressive governments.

I sometimes wonder what the imperialists teach in their military training centres in the way of "loyalty"—surely one of the basic qualities of a good soldier. The record of treason among those who have passed through their courses of training is prodigious. Afrifa is a fair example.

Approximately one-sixth of Ghana's officer corps were trained at Sandhurst, though for some years we had been sending an increasing number to train in the Soviet Union and in other socialist countries. It is significant that not one of the officers trained in the Soviet Union took part in the February rising.

Throughout the independent states of Africa there are foreign military missions and training schemes which involve the indoctrination of our young armies with imperialist ideas and traditions. It is estimated that in 1964 nearly 3,000 French officers and men were seconded or contracted to the armed forces of the independent African states, while 1,500 Africans were training in France. Recently the United States has greatly increased its military expenditure and activity in Africa. In 1964-65 U.S. aid to the Congo (Kinshasa) quadrupled that of Belgium. Liberia and Ethiopia are also receiving large-scale American military "aid". Growing numbers of African officers are being sent for training in the U.S.A. and West Germany.

Over the years, links have been forged between army officers of different African states who have received training in the same or similar overseas military establishments. These links have been strengthened by organisations such as the Defence Commission of the Organisation of African Unity (O.A.U.), the Equatorial Defence Council and the Afro-Malagasy Defence Organisation. One coup could therefore tend to spark off another.

The arrogant, ambitious "élite" of imperialist-trained officers among our professional armies have already caused much suffering and confusion in Africa. They have been the willing tools of neo-colonialists and of reactionary, counter-revolutionary forces within their own countries. In a rash of army mutinies and coups between the end of 1962 and March 1967 fifteen African Heads of State have been removed and the positions of others seriously endangered.

The only way to ensure against the possibility of internal subversion carried out by the army and inspired and aided by outside forces is eventually, when an All-African Union Government has been established, to abolish professional armies altogether and to build instead a people's militia, by arming the peasants and urban workers, as in China and Cuba. Such an armed force cannot be subverted and is the best guardian of the people's interests and welfare.

We were moving towards the establishment of a people's militia in Ghana, and this is one of the reasons why there was support among certain army officers for a seizure of power. They feared competition from the militia and the Presidential Guard Regiment, thinking I was building up a "private army". Kotoka admitted this when he visited New York to consult his masters some months after the setting up of the "N.L.C." "Nkrumah," he said, "was building a militia. Who can tolerate that?"

Record of Military Action in Africa, December 1962—March 1967

17th December 1962	Senegal	Attempt to overthrow President Senghor. Failed.
13th January 1963	Togo	Assassination of President Olympio
12th-15th August 1963	Brazzaville	Forced resignation of President Youlou.
19th-28th October 1963	Dahomey	President Hubert Maga deposed.
3rd December 1963	Niamey	Military mutiny. Suppressed by President Hamani Diori.
20th, 23rd, 24th January 1964	Tanzania Uganda Kenya	Military mutinies. Suppressed with aid of British troops.
18th February 1964	Gabon	President Leon M'ba deposed.
18th June 1965	Algeria	President Ben Bella overthrown.
25th November 1965	Congo (Leo)	Presidential powers assumed by General Mobutu.
22nd December 1965	Dahomey	Assumption of power by General Soglo.
1st January 1965	Central African Republic	Forced resignation of President David Dacko.
4th January 1965	Upper Volta	President Yameogo deposed.
15th January 1966	Nigeria	Federal Prime Minister Balewa and two regional premiers killed (General Ironsi in power).
24th February 1966	Ghana	Seizure of power by neo-colonialist inspired army and police officers.

29th July 1966	Nigeria	General Ironsi killed. General Gowon in power.
29th November 1966	Burundi	King Ntare V deposed.
13th January 1967	Togo	Forced resignation of President Grunitzky.
24th March 1967	Sierra Leone	Army seizure of power.

Nearly all these military interventions were counter-revolutionary in character and have set the clock back in the states in which they occurred. It seemed for a time as though Africa might be going the same way as Latin America. Obviously the precise course of the military action in each territory differed, but most of them had certain factors in common which give the clue to their true nature and origin. In each case where there has been counter-revolutionary armed action there has been a link-up between foreign-trained army officers, local reactionary opposition elements and imperialists and neo-colonialists.

Ten of the 38 independent states of Africa now have military regimes established as a result of "coups". These military so-called governments administer some 99 million people. The neo-colonialists smile: the peoples of Africa suffer. But the African Revolution triumphs.

As I said in my sessional address to the National Assembly in Accra on 1st February 1966: "It is not the duty of the army to rule or govern, because it has no political mandate and its duty is not to seek a political mandate. The army only operates under the mandate of the civil government. If the national interest compels the armed forces to intervene, then immediately after the intervention the army must hand over to a new civil government elected by the people and enjoying the people's mandate under a constitution accepted by them. If the army does not do this then the position of the army becomes dubious and anomalous, and involves a betrayal of the people and the national interest."

For some years, imperialism has had its back to the wall in Africa. It has been faced with a growing liberation movement which it is powerless to stop but which, if it allows it to go unchecked, will before long end the exploitation on which imperialism's very existence depends. It has therefore resorted to a co-ordinated strategy in an attempt to preserve, and if

48

possible to extend, its grip on the economic life of our continent.

An all-out offensive is being waged against the progressive, independent states. Where the more subtle methods of economic pressure and political subversion have failed to achieve the desired result, there has been resort to violence in order to promote a change of regime and prepare the way for the establishment of a puppet government.

Fragmented into so many separate states, many of them weak and economically non-viable, coup d'états have been relatively easy to arrange in Africa. All that has been needed was a small force of disciplined men to seize the key points of the capital city and to arrest the existing political leadership. In the planning and carrying out of these coups there have always been just sufficient numbers of dissatisfied and ambitious army officers and politicians willing to co-operate to make the whole operation possible.

It has been one of the tasks of the C.I.A. and other similar organisations to discover these potential quislings and traitors in our midst, and to encourage them, by bribery and the promise of political power, to destroy the constitutional government of their countries. In Ghana the embassies of the United States, Britain, and West Germany were all implicated in the plot to overthrow my government. It is alleged that the U.S. Ambassador, Franklin Williams, offered the traitors 13 million dollars to carry out a coup d'état. Afrifa, Harlley and Kotoka were to get a large share of this if they would assassinate me at Accra airport as I prepared to leave for Hanoi. I understand Afrifa said: "I think I will fail", and declined the offer. So apparently did the others.

It is particularly disgraceful that it should have been an Afro-American ambassador who sold himself out to the imperialists and allowed himself to be used in this way. It was this same man who deliberately lied when he publicly described the coup as "bloodless." However, his treachery provides a sharp reminder of the insidious ways in which the enemies of Africa can operate. In the U.S.A. the "Uncle Tom" figure is well known. We have mercifully seen less of him in Africa.

The activities of the C.I.A. no longer surprise us. We have experienced many examples of the work of this organisation in recent years. Last May (1966) the subversive activities of the U.S. Embassy military attaché in Somalia, Colonel Rozmer, were exposed. He had been making approaches to Somali army officers and had organised the illegal importation of arms into the country with the object of carrying out a coup d'état. In July 1965 Taylor Odell, an attaché of the U.S. embassy, was expelled from Egypt after being caught red-handed receiving confidential documents from Mustafa Amin, an Egyptian C.I.A. agent. In South Sudan, the so-called Azana Liberation Front was founded with C.I.A. support and funds. Its purpose was to detach South Sudan from the rest of the country and to proclaim an independent state of Azana. In the Congo (Brazzaville) the C.I.A. has been involved in various attempts to sabotage the progressive government of President Massemba-Debat. The record of C.I.A. activity in the Congo (Kinshasa) is equally disturbing and continuing.

Between 1961 and 1964, C.I.A. agents murdered a number of politicians and important public men in Burundi; the last being the Prime Minister of that country, Pierre Ngendandumwe, whose assassin, C.I.A. agent Gonzalve Muyenzi, worked as an accountant in the U.S. embassy. When his flat was searched, 3,000,000 francs were discovered which Muyenzi had received from the C.I.A. Having disposed of Ngendandumwe, pressure from the U.S. compelled the new Burundi government to refuse help to the Congolese nationalists whose victory the C.I.A. believed would obstruct U.S. activities in the Congo.

The C.I.A. was deeply implicated in the attempted coup in Tanzania in 1964. It paid lavishly for the services of a number of Tanzanian politicians.

Further examples of C.I.A. activity and the work of other foreign intelligence organisations in Africa could be given. They would provide material for a book of their own. As I write here in Conakry, I have just learned that five C.I.A. experts have arrived in Liberia to find out how I manage to communicate with my supporters inside Ghana. Doubtless they have been called in by the puppet "N.L.C." whose creation owed so much to U.S. and British Intelligence.

Dean Rusk, U.S. Secretary of State, at a meeting of 150 American top businessmen in June 1966, predicted that the "downfall" of President Ben Bella, President Sukarno and myself would be followed by the overthrow of more left-wing world leaders. He started to name them, but thought better of it, and ended his predictions with an enigmatic smile.

We know both the strength and the limitations of imperialist intelligence organisations. While being responsible for a great deal of the unrest in Africa in recent years, they have not been as successful as many would have us believe. This is partly because they have frequently been outwitted by the superior techniques and organisation of certain counter-intelligence services. It is also due to the fact that they have failed in many instances to buy the co-operation of a sufficient number of key Africans who are prepared to betray their countrymen, and on whose sell-out they depend ultimately for their success.

In Ghana, Harlley, Kotoka, Afrifa and Deku were just the kind of men they were looking for. It was when all had been arranged and the army and police seizure of power was about to take place that Ankrah was finally approached and without a thought he replied in one word: "Mafé", which in the Ga language means "I will do it."

4

"OPPOSITION" ELEMENTS

The members of the "old opposition" with whom the
"N.L.C." are closely associated, are the same people who
tried to sabotage the winning of our political independence ten
years ago. They struck on 24th February 1966, just as we were
about to break through and win our economic independence.
In January 1966, we had inaugurated the first electricity from
the Volta dam; and only three days before their treachery, I
had signed a new agreement to irrigate the mighty Accra
plains. Ghana was all set for a tremendous march forward into
a new industrial era, and a great expansion in our food growing capacity. This was the moment for which we had worked
so hard. And this was the time this small group of unpatriotic
selfish men, egged on by their neo-colonialist masters, chose
to strike.

They shouted from the rooftops that they acted spontane-
ously to save Ghana from "economic chaos". But as everyone
who has studied the history of Ghana over the last fifteen years
or so knows, their action was only the culmination of a whole
series of actions aimed against my government and against
myself. They have a long record of go-slow policies, of subversive activity and of alignment with imperialists and their
agents. Unable to gain victory at the polls they even resorted
to assassination plots in order to impose themselves on the
people of Ghana, and to avenge their political defeat.

It is these same people who became members of the political
committee set up by the "N.L.C." in June 1966. Nearly all
were supporters of the former United Party, an amorphous
group of people who for various reasons opposed my government. The chairman of the political committee, Edward
Akuffo-Addo, was a well-known member of the United Party;
Kofi Busia, deputy chairman, was its leader. Like their Sand-

52

hurst counterparts, these members of the civilian political committee are deeply imbued with British traditions. Most of them received at least part of their education in Britain. They returned to their native country as if in blinkers, seeing and judging everything in Oxbridge terms. They saw the liberation struggle as a movement to be conducted slowly and "respectably" by themselves, the professional and intellectual élite, and as having nothing to do with the toiling masses whom they regarded with a mixture of fear and scorn.

It was men such as these, George Grant, J. B. Danquah, Ofori Atta, Akuffo Addo, Ako Adjei and Obetsebi Lamptey, who were the nucleus of the United Gold Coast Convention (U.G.C.C.), the organisation I launched in Saltpond on 29th December 1947 to achieve independence "by all legitimate and constitutional means." Danquah, a vice-president of the U.G.C.C., was one of the original supporters of the unpopular Burns Constitution. In fact, right from the start, the U.G.C.C. lacked popular support, and it was partly in order to make it appear a movement of the people that I was invited to become its general secretary. I had then spent ten years studying in the U.S.A., and was in England taking up further studies at the London School of Economics, and at University College, but spending a large part of my time at the West African National Secretariat and the West African Students Union (W.A.S.U.), organisations dedicated to the achievement of West African unity and the liquidation of colonialism. I also spent a lot of time helping to organise the Colonial Workers Association of Great Britain.

Danquah wrote personally to me urging me to accept the appointment. I was at first reluctant, having heard that the promoters of the U.G.C.C. were out of touch with the people, and were mainly middle-class reactionary lawyers and budding capitalists with whom, with my revolutionary background, I would be out of sympathy. But on the advice of the West African National Secretariat I agreed, and returned home on 16th December 1947 after an absence of twelve years.

Within 18 months of my return I was compelled to dissociate myself from the slow-moving and restricted U.G.C.C. and to form a new party, the Convention People's Party. This party, based on the support of the broad masses of the people and of the youth, demanded "self-government NOW", unlike

53

the U.G.C.C. which asked for self-government "within the shortest possible time". I proclaimed the formation of the C.P.P. before a crowd of some 60,000 people in Accra stadium on 12th June 1949. The leaders of the U.G.C.C. never forgave me. They became implacable opponents of the Party, determined to obstruct its progress at every stage, and to attack me personally on all possible occasions.

They showed their hand almost immediately after the birth of the Party, when I was summoned to appear before a special meeting of the Ga State Council, the Accra traditional local authority, to explain what I meant by "Positive Action". Ex-members of the Working Committee of the U.G.C.C. were there in force at the meeting and pressed to have me banished from Accra. They blamed me for what they described as the growing "lawlessness" in the country, though what they really feared was the evidence of the political awakening of the people.

I explained to the meeting that at that particular stage of our struggle, positive action entailed non-violent methods such as press campaigns, strikes, boycotts and other forms of non-co-operation. That very night, I wrote and printed on my little Cropper machine a pamphlet called "What I mean by Positive Action", so that there should be no doubt in anyone's mind about the legitimate and constitutional means by which we intended at that time to attack the forces of imperialism in the country, should the Coussey Report on constitutional reform, which was about to be published, prove unsatisfactory. It was this Cropper machine which was used to print the *Accra Evening News*.

But my long-standing political opponents chose to invent their own interpretation of "What I mean by Positive Action" and labelled me a dangerous rabble-rouser advocating violence.

As expected, the Coussey Report published at the end of October 1949 was completely unsatisfactory. I therefore called together the representatives of over 50 national organisations to meet in the Ghana People's Representative Assembly on 20th November, to oppose the Report and to decide on effective action. The Assembly resolved "that the Coussey Report and His Majesty's Government's statement thereto are unacceptable to the country as a whole" and declared "that the people of the Gold Coast be granted immediate self-government". With typical lack of concern for the country's progress, the executive committee of the U.G.C.C. did not attend the Assembly, and afterwards, the chiefs at Dodowah, led by Nana Ofori Atta II, stated that they did not accept the views of the Assembly.

Later, when I had launched the campaign for positive action, and it was really beginning to take effect, the Joint Provincial Council of Chiefs joined with the colonial government in attempting to suppress the campaign. At a meeting of the Joint Provincial Council of Chiefs I explained the need to continue positive action until the rank and file of the people were permitted, through the election of a constituent assembly, to express their views on constitutional reform. It was like speaking to a brick wall. Danquah's declaration, that "those who go against constitutional authority must expect to pay for it with their neck", sums up the defeatist attitude of these people, and explains how they never managed to lead a genuine and popular liberation movement.

Instead of supporting the efforts of the man in the street to express himself and to bring pressure to bear on the imperialists, these political opponents of the Party ranged themselves on the side of the British colonial government in trying to suppress the great upsurge of nationalism.

They condoned and even assisted in a wave of arrests of key supporters of the Party and leaders in the campaign of positive action. Kojo Botsio, general secretary of the Party, was arrested on 17th January 1950. My own arrest followed shortly afterwards.

I was sentenced to a total of three years' imprisonment, two years for attempting to "coerce the government of the Gold Coast" by launching the campaign of positive action, and the third year for "sedition" as publisher of the *Daily Mail* in which a "seditious" article had appeared. In fact, I only served 14 months. In the general election of 8th February 1951, the Party won a sweeping victory and I was elected as member of the Legislative Assembly for Accra Central. The colonial government had no choice but to release me. I left prison on 12th February, and on the request of the Governor of the Gold Coast, Sir Charles Arden-Clarke, formed a government and became Leader of Government Business. At once I

55

proclaimed that our great task was to press ahead with the struggle for "self-government now". And once again, members of the Opposition went into action to try to wreck the independence movement.

Disgruntled at the success of the Party in the general election, and disappointed at not receiving positions in the new government, they proceeded to try to cause confusion and discontent among the people by announcing that now we had landed ourselves "good jobs" we had forsaken the policy of "self-government now". I challenged our political opponents to join us in a campaign of positive action in order to achieve "self-government now". I invited Danquah, Lamptey and the Executive of the U.G.C.C.; Ollenu, Bossman and the Executive of the National Democratic Party; the chiefs of the Asanteman Council; Nana Ofori Atta I, President of the Joint Provincial Council and chiefs of that Council; Kobina Sekyi, and the Executive of the Aborigines Rights Protection Society —all our critics, to notify the General Secretary of the Party in conference to plan a nation-wide campaign of positive action if the British government rejected a motion for "self-government now".

The sincerity of our political opponents and their connivance with the colonial government may be judged by the fact that not one of them answered the challenge.

A few years later, after the 1954 general election, when the Party won 72 out of the 104 seats in the Legislative Assembly, the largest anti-government party was the Northern People's Party which had 12 seats. The remaining 20 opposition members were mostly Independents, several of whom later attached themselves to one party or another. The anti-government members of the Assembly did not then constitute an opposition in the accepted sense of the term, since there was no group among them capable of forming an alternative government. They were therefore recognised simply as a body of critics of my government—an unofficial opposition.

Before long, however, the members of the unofficial opposition decided to amalgamate and to form a single party—the National Liberation Movement (N.L.M.). The reader will note the close analogy in the name of the N.L.M. and the "N.L.C.", both of which had about as little to do with "liberation" as it is possible to imagine.

The circumstances which led to the formation of the N.L.M. illustrate its reactionary nature and its negative policies. It was formed shortly after the introduction of the Cocoa Duty and Development Funds (Amendment) Bill into the Assembly in August 1954. The purpose of the Bill was to fix the price paid to cocoa farmers at 72 shillings a load (62 lb.) for four years, the duration of that Assembly.

This measure was needed to avoid inflation. Demand for cocoa in the world market had far exceeded the supply, and the price had risen to a record height. If the price paid locally to the farmers was increased proportionately, our Development Plan would be jeopardised by the inevitable rise in prices of consumer goods which would be followed by a demand for wage and salary increases. My government, therefore, under the terms of the proposed Bill guaranteed to pay the cocoa farmers 72 shillings a load irrespective of how low the world price of cocoa might fall during the ensuing four years, and to use any funds that accrued to expand the economy of the country as a whole.

The cocoa farmers in general reacted favourably to the Bill, but our political opponents seized the opportunity of fanning tribal and regional friction in order to attack us. All the remnants of various parties which had been formed at one time or another in opposition to my government joined together in the "Council for Higher Cocoa Prices". This organisation however, did not last long, and it was succeeded by the National Liberation Movement, which adopted as its *raison d'etre* the demand for a federal form of government. By linking the cocoa question with the idea of federation, members of the N.L.M. tried to spread discontent throughout Ashanti. They alleged that the Cocoa Bill was unjust to the cocoa farmers, and that Ashanti would be better off managing its own affairs and spending all the income from cocoa within Ashanti instead of contributing to the general development of the country. In this campaign to spread discontent and disunity, the N.L.M. were assisted by the Asanteman Council, headed by the Asantehene. For a time there was much violence in Ashanti, and hundreds of Ashanti Party members were forced to take refuge in Accra and other parts of the country.

At this time, as on former and later occasions, the imperialist press supported the opposition and gave an entirely false impression of the state of the country. The object was to spread the idea that my policies were causing widespread bloodshed, and that we were not ready for independence. Already, the opposition had become very dependent on imperialist support, and therefore deeply implicated in its policies. They had a common interest in trying to undermine my government and to prevent the successful implementation of its political, economic and social programme.

It was no mere coincidence that the first attempt to be made on my life occurred while the trouble in Ashanti, stirred up by the opposition, was at its height. It took place on the evening of 10th November 1955, while I was working at home. There were two large explosions which shattered all the windows, but no one was injured. I learned afterwards that enough gelignite was used to have destroyed the house entirely and to have killed everyone in it, but that it had been inadequately prepared and badly placed. The police made half-hearted enquiries, and no arrests were made.

During the next few months, the opposition stepped up its agitation for a federal form of government, though it is doubtful if they could sincerely have thought this suitable in a country of nearly 100,000 square miles, with a population then of under six million. However, full consideration was given to their demand and every effort was made to reach an understanding. The leaders of the N.L.M. were invited by four members of the Legislative Assembly, two of whom represented constituencies in Kumasi, to discuss the matter at a round-table conference. They refused on the ground that the suggestion did not come directly from the government. I therefore, sent an official government invitation. This they refused. In the hope that they might change their mind I sent yet another invitation. They again turned it down.

I introduced a Motion in the Assembly on 5th April 1955, calling for the appointment of a Select Committee to examine the whole question of the suitability of a federal system of government. Although the opposition was entitled to have only two members on the Committee, as against seven from the government benches, I agreed to allow them to nominate five. In spite of this concession, the leader of the opposition declared that they would not co-operate, and he and his 20 supporters walked out of the Assembly just after the Motion had been seconded. The excuse they gave for boy-cotting the Select Committee was a strange one. They said they did not consider the Committee competent to deal with national matters, and this regardless of the fact that it was composed entirely of members of the national Legislative Assembly.

The Select Committee consisting of 12 members including the Chairman, C. H. Chapman the Deputy Speaker, held 22 meetings and considered 299 written memoranda and 60 other written statements before issuing its report on 26th July, in which it advised against a federal form of government. It recommended that regional councils should be set up to which certain powers and functions of the central government should be delegated.

The opposition, still dissatisfied, determined to try to delay the independence issue indefinitely by continuing to oppose everything the government proposed. Whenever the question of the constitution was raised in the Assembly they walked out.

Undoubtedly, they gained much encouragement to persist in their obstructionist attitude by the support they obtained from the British government and press, which, although paying lip service to "democracy", has always in Africa where it suited their interests shown far more concern for minority rights than for the rights of the majority. Much publicity was given to the unrest in Ashanti and to opposition views, the subjects being discussed at length in both Houses of Parliament. But practically no publicity or sympathy was shown for the wishes of the overwhelming majority of the people of the Gold Coast who had demonstrated quite clearly that they supported the Party and a unitary form of government.

In a further effort to resolve the constitutional issue, I asked for and received a mandate from the Legislative Assembly to invite the British government to send a constitutional adviser to help formulate a suitable constitution and to advise on the devolution of certain powers to the Regions. Sir Frederick Bourne was sent. For nearly three months he travelled in every part of the country and discussed constitutional problems with every organisation and individual who wished to see him. But when he visited Kumasi to meet the leaders of the N.L.M. and their supporters, he found that they did not wish to see him. The excuse for their unwillingness to take part in any discussions on the constitution was that the government had, in November 1955, passed the State Councils (Ashanti) Amendment Bill. This Bill permitted those chiefs who had been destooled by the Asanteman Council the right to appeal to the Governor. Several chiefs had been destooled in Ashanti by the Asanteman Council for no other reason than that they were supporters of the government and against the federalist idea. Under the then existing laws they had no right of appeal. Clearly this was a matter which needed attention, and the State Councils Bill was designed to put an end to this victimisation.

Sir Frederick Bourne, in his Report, recommended the devolution of certain powers and functions to the Regional Assemblies, but that all legislation should be enacted by the central authority. I thereupon convened a conference of all the principal representative bodies and organisations in the country to meet at Achimota on 16th February 1956, to discuss Bourne's Report and other matters affecting the form of the constitution. Once again, the N.L.M. and its allies refused to participate. The conference was adjourned for a week to enable delegates from the Joint Provincial Council of Chiefs to persuade them to attend. But their mission failed. The delegates tried again later, but were still unsuccessful in getting the opposition elements to participate. The result was, that although the conference agreed almost all the recommendations of Sir Frederick Bourne its findings were not acceptable to the British Secretary of State as providing the necessary conditions for the granting of a firm date for independence, since the N.L.M. had not taken part in the discussions. Once more, the old alliance of the opposition and the imperialists had demonstrated their common interest in trying to delay independence.

I therefore drew up my own constitutional proposals for the sovereign and independent state of "Ghana," and put them before the Assembly on 15th May 1956. The motion was debated and passed on 5th June, after which the Assembly was dissolved and a general election declared, to take place in July. The British Secretary of State gave the pledge:

> "If a General Election is held, Her Majesty's Government will be ready to accept a Motion calling for

Independence within the Commonwealth passed by a reasonable majority in a newly elected Legislature and then to declare a firm date for attainment of their purpose."

The election was to be the final test of opinion for or against a federation. The outcome would show just how much or how little support the political opponents of the Party really had in the country.

The result was decisive. The Party won 71 seats, increased later by the support of one of the Independents, which gave a majority of 40 in the Legislative Assembly. Unlike the N.L.M., the Party won seats throughout the country as a whole, and was the only Party which could claim to speak in a national sense. Even in Ashanti, then the stronghold of the N.L.M., the Party won 8 out of the 21 seats and received 43 per cent of the votes cast, an increase on the previous election.

The reaction of Busia to the decisive election result was to call a press conference in Kumasi and to declare that the election had established the opposition case for a federation, since the Party had not won overall majorities in Ashanti and the Northern Territories. His action staggered even some of his closest colleagues. Everyone knew that the election had been fought on the federation issue and that the Party had won more than a "reasonable majority". Furthermore, during the course of the election campaign, Busia himself had declared that he would be prepared to form a government if the N.L.M. secured anything over 52 members. That is, he had accepted the fact that a single overall majority, even of one seat, constituted a democratic verdict.

When the new Assembly was formally opened, the opposition benches were empty except for two members who turned up from Togoland. Afterwards, Busia and his friends excused themselves by saying that they arrived late and could not get through the dense crowds outside the Assembly.

The Governor, in his speech at the opening ceremony, stated that the government would that week introduce a Bill declaring the Gold Coast a sovereign and independent state within the Commonwealth. The following day the opposition tabled an amendment criticising the proposal as "premature" until a further effort had been made to get "an agreed Constitution."

The amendment was defeated by a majority of 37. Where-upon, adopting their old tactics, the opposition issued a statement to the press saying they would absent themselves from the Assembly when the Independence Motion came before the House. Busia, showing where his real support lay, announced that he considered the struggle centred not in the Gold Coast but in London, and that the opposition would send a delegation to the British government.

As I recall these times, when the opposition persistently refused either to participate in national discussions or to respect the decision of the great majority of the people, I wonder how they managed to retain even the little support they had. Their actions were so unpatriotic, dishonest and undignified. They aligned themselves with those who wished to retard the country's progress towards independence. At the same time, while loudly proclaiming their belief in democracy, they were prepared to try to force the will of a small minority on the majority of the nation, and so make a farce of parliamentary government.

Busia who led the opposition delegation to London, actually appealed to the British government not to grant independence. He said the country was not ready for it: "We still need you (the British) in the Gold Coast." I imagine he would say today that the Americans were needed! He found some support among sections of the British press, but there could be no denying that the conditions laid down by the Secretary of State, that my motion for independence should be passed by "a reasonable majority in the newly elected Legislature", had been satisfied, and at long last a date for independence was fixed—the 6th of March 1957.

The long struggle to achieve our political freedom was over. But in a sense our task of building a really independent Ghana was only just beginning. Political independence was incomplete without economic independence, and as I said in the midnight pronouncement of independence in Accra on 6th March 1957, "the independence of Ghana is meaningless unless it is linked up with the total liberation of the African continent".

My government, therefore, was pledged to the twin task of achieving economic independence for Ghana, and of participating in the wider African revolution. The former implied the adoption of socialist policies, since in the African situation genuine independence is incompatible with capitalism; while the latter involved us in actively supporting the liberation and unity movements in Africa. In both these tasks, my government immediately came up against opposition from the same quarters as before, that is, from reactionary bourgeois elements inside Ghana, and from imperialist and neo-colonialist interests outside. As before, these forces had a common interest; both wished to delay economic independence and to impede the progress of the African revolution. The tactics they employed were suitably adjusted to the new situation.

After 1957, having been repeatedly rejected by the electorate, the opposition lost hope of gaining office by constitutional means, and embarked on a campaign of obstructing the work of government without making any attempt to devise an alternative programme. They asserted themselves outside the democratic framework. Their policies, always regional in concept, became purely destructive, subversive and violent. Before independence they had been prepared to sacrifice our national liberation in order to keep me and my colleagues out of government; now they were ready to sabotage our newly-born freedom and to hold up the African revolution by allying themselves even more closely with imperialists and the insidious forces of neo-colonialism in causing a breakdown in administration so that they might get a chance to grasp the reins of office.

They employed every stratagem, from demanding the virtual secession of Ashanti, the Northern Region and Togoland from the sphere of Central Ghanaian authority, to a press campaign of abuse and lies to discredit me and the government. When this failed, they resorted to violence, assassination plots, and eventually to the subversion of army and police officers.

For a time after 1957 we tolerated the excesses of the opposition, but when their actions began to undermine the state and to jeopardise its independence we took measures, like all governments do in times of national emergency, to ensure the security of the nation. For example, we brought in the Avoidance of Discrimination Bill to deal with the control of political parties based on tribal and religious affiliations. Its effect was to cause the various opposition parties to join together into a single party, the United Party. Later, after two and a half years of putting up with a vicious opposition press campaign, certain restrictions were placed on the press; and a fifth attempt on my life made preventive detention necessary. By then, assassination attempts had resulted in the death of 30 Ghanaians, men, women and children, and the wounding of some 300 others.

We could not allow a small minority of unprincipled men to continue to stir up disunity and confusion with the object of overthrowing the government, which had the support of the overwhelming majority of the people of Ghana, support shown decisively in the general election before independence and in the 1964 referendum which established the C.P.P. as the national party of Ghana. Maximum unity and effort was vital if my government was successfully to carry out its mandate of reconstruction and development.

A distinction must be made between the loss of freedom to subvert, and the loss of freedom of expression. At no time has my government denied the right of Ghanaians to hold political meetings and to discuss the country's affairs with complete frankness. In the National Assembly, as the official reports show, debates were vigorous and unrestricted; members did not hesitate to criticise and expose social wrongs and injustices. Visitors to Ghana from non-socialist countries often spoke to me of their surprise at hearing politics discussed freely and openly throughout the country, when they had been led to believe that the one-party system stifled political differences and made any kind of criticism impossible. There were wide differences of opinion within the Party, and members were always encouraged to say what they thought on all aspects of the government's policy. It has been said by a Western observer that "within the C.P.P. there were as wide political differences and antagonisms as those existing in Britain". The point I wish to make is that under our system of democratic centralism, criticism comes from within and is constructive. The people of Ghana when they established a one-party state in the 1964 constitutional referendum were merely giving *de jure* recognition to an established fact.

The two party system has shown itself to be unsuitable in any African state. It has grown up in Britain to serve specific class interests. It was perhaps our fault that we did not realise this sooner and attempt earlier to build the type of one party state most suited to our needs. The Sierra Leonean army had exactly the same social background and British training as that of Ghana and yet carried out its coup d'état to suppress the two party system. Indeed, the excuse offered by the Sierra Leonean rebels was that their action was forced on them by the failure of the two party system.

The first priority in Ghana at the time of independence was to make use of our pitifully small stock of professional and technical experts. Whatever their political views they had to be utilised to the full in the interest of the newly emerged Ghana state. From the start I had to bring not only into my cabinet but had to appoint to important posts in the judiciary, the civil service and the universities, individuals who had been active opponents of the Party in colonial days.

We could not afford to do without such few qualified African doctors, accountants, architects, engineers, university teachers and professional people generally as were available immediately after independence. A formula had to be found by which they could not only be employed in state service and in development generally but brought within the Party. This in its turn meant that the Party itself could not in these conditions restrict itself to those who understood and had practised a socialist ideology. The calculated risk of admitting these persons to our organisation was one we had to take. Nevertheless, these colonial trained professional classes, with certain notable exceptions, looked on independence as a strictly national concern. In many cases, all they were concerned with was taking the places of the former colonial occupiers of their jobs and making the same money as these did in the same social and economic pattern. Insofar as they were within the Party they were a source of weakness because they sabotaged attempts to prevent corruption and, in a number of cases, actually joined in it themselves. Yet if they had been excluded from the Party, they would have joined the so-called "opposition" which had become, almost from the moment of independence, a purely conspiratorial organisation.

In the same way I had to try to accommodate within the Party the leaders of traditional society, the chiefs.

On reflection even though I trusted too much in the power

65

of a reformed chieftaincy I was not mistaken in attempting to use popularly chosen chiefs within the framework of the government. It was then essential to have the broadest possible grouping of interests at home if we were to be sufficiently united to deal with the external issue, namely, the political unification of the African continent.

I could have dismissed many of the higher police officers about whose loyalty I had doubts. But whom could I have put in their place? So little education was done in colonial times that actual illiteracy was a major problem in the army and police. Were it not for the continued criminal conspiracy by the opposition then I might have taken the risk of abolishing the Special Branch at an earlier stage. After all, it was not even a part of the old colonial set-up and had only been instituted to deal with me and the C.P.P. in 1949. If I had done so, however, all security would have had to be entrusted to the Party and while I did use it as a major source of information as to what was taking place in the country, once again it would have been equally dangerous to have relied exclusively on it.

I had to combat not only tribalism but the African tradition that a man's first duty was to his family group and that therefore nepotism was the highest of all virtues. While I believe we had largely eliminated tribalism as an active force, its by-products and those of the family system were still with us. I could not have chosen my government without some regard to tribal origins and even, within the Party itself, there was at times a tendency to condemn or recommend some individual on the basis of his tribal or family origin. Dangerous and defective as the police investigation system was, it did at least provide me with a second opinion from individuals trained, at any rate in theory, to give objective judgments.

Further, the necessarily broad nature of the Party made some of its wealthier members quite willing to use its machinery for private ends and to discredit police officers or civil servants who were looking too closely into their affairs. Of tribal and family groups there were even those within it who might be prepared to recommend for detention individuals who took the opposite side to themselves in the election of a chief or in the running of traditional affairs.

The issues we faced at independence were so gigantic that within every sphere we had to take calculated risks. We could not, however obvious were the limitations of many of the police, the civil service and the judiciary, change them overnight. We had had no revolutionary war which would have produced and trained those who might take their place.

The problems we faced at independence were similar to those which confront most states emerging from colonialism. A once dependent territory if it is to survive in the modern world must try to accomplish in a single generation what it has taken developed nations 300 years or more to achieve. There is need for radical change in practically every department of national life. For example, after a people's revolution it is essential that the top ranks of the Armed Forces, Police and Civil Service be filled by men who believe in the ideology of the Revolution, and not by those whose loyalties remain with the old order.

In most cases, the whole economy of the country has to be reorganised, agriculture diversified, industries started from scratch, harbours, roads, airports built, and crash programmes of education inaugurated to cope with the sudden and increasing demand for skilled technicians and administrators. In this great undertaking there can be no place for slackers or saboteurs.

The one-party system of government is now the accepted pattern of government in a large part of independent Africa. But when we were evolving this form it was relatively new, and it was loudly condemned by our enemies. As I told members of the National Assembly in my Sessional Address on 1st February 1966: "A one-party system of government is an effective and safe instrument only when it operates in a socialist society. In other words, it must be a political expression of the will of the masses working for the ultimate good and welfare of the people as a whole. On the other hand, a one-party system of government in a neo-colonialist client state, subject to external pressures and control, can quickly develop into the most dangerous form of tyranny, despotism and oppression. It can become in the hands of a few privileged rascally-minded and selfish individuals in a neo-colonialist state a weapon and tool for suppressing the legitimate aspirations of the people in the interests of foreign powers and their agents. I repeat, a one-party state can only function for the good of the people within the framework of a socialist state or in a developing state with a socialist programme. The government governs through the people, and not through class cleavages and interests. In other words, the basis of government is the will of the people."

The capitalist-imperialist world is still explaining the tension in the world today in terms of a conflict between "dictatorship" and "democracy"; the first is equated with communism and tyranny, the latter with enlightenment and freedom. In this way, imperialist and neo-colonialists seek to conceal the true content of the struggle which lies in the reaction between capitalism and socialism.

We expected opposition to our development plans from the relics of the old "opposition", from the Anglophile intellectual and professional élite, and of course, from neo-colonialists who viewed the obvious signs of our approaching economic independence with growing alarm. What we did not perhaps anticipate sufficiently was the backsliding of some of our own party members, men like Gbedemah and Adamafio, who for reasons of personal ambition, and because they only paid lip-service to socialism, sought to destroy the Party.

Right from the foundation of the Party, as everyone in Ghana knows, I have waged a ceaseless war against corruption. In the "Dawn Broadcast" made on 8th April 1961, I stressed the need to eliminate it from our society: "I am aware that the evil of patronage finds a good deal of place in our society. I consider that it is entirely wrong for persons placed in positions of eminence or authority to use the influence of office in patronising others, in many cases wrong persons, for immoral favours. I am seeing to it that this evil shall be uprooted, no matter whose ox is gored. The same thing goes for nepotism, which is, so to speak, a twin brother of the evil of patronage . . . . It is most important to remember that the strength of the Convention People's Party derives from the masses of the people. These men and women include those whom I have constantly referred to as the unknown warriors —dedicated men and women who serve the Party loyally and selflessly without hoping for reward. It is therefore natural for the masses to feel some resentment when they see comrades whom they have put into power and have given the mandate to serve the country on their behalf, begin to forget themselves and indulge in ostentatious living. High Party officials, Ministers, Ministerial Secretaries, Chairmen of statutory boards and corporations must forever bear this in mind. Some of us very easily forget that we ourselves have risen from amongst the masses."

My difficulty was to get the police to enforce the principles I laid down. It was only when I personally supervised the direction of criminal investigation against ministers and prominent Party members that anything was done. For example, a former Minister of Agriculture, F. Y. Asare, was involved with one Kojo Djaba and a civil service accomplice, and was convicted. Even this case would never have come before the courts if I had not personally set up a special body independent of the police to investigate it.

It is significant that the Judge who tried this particular case was the first of those to be dismissed by the "N.L.C.", even before they got rid of the Chief Justice; and after the 'coup' Asare and his confederates had their convictions annulled by the "N.L.C." constituted Appeal Court.

Sufficient time has now elapsed to show that the "N.L.C." never seriously wished to investigate corruption. Had they done so it would have involved too many of their own members. It was a propaganda device directed against my own government, making use of the fact that there were a number of instances of corruption among ministers and Party officials. Unlike in Asare's case, these had not been dealt with because the police themselves could not furnish the evidence. The attitude of the "N.L.C." is shown by the fact that when I had mentioned in a broadcast from Guinea that Harlley and Deku were involved in diamond smuggling and challenged the "N.L.C." to set up an enquiry into diamond racketeering in Ghana the Commission which they were thus forced to establish sat in secret and no report by it was ever issued.

This purely propaganda approach is even better illustrated in my own case. I am alleged to have "stolen" millions. In fact I have no money outside Ghana except for the sums which have been paid to me after the 'coup' as royalties on my books and which are now paid into the London Branch of the National Commercial Bank of Scotland.

I never handled any money personally for any external or internal purposes and this included my own salary. All drawing both on governmental and my personal accounts was counter-signed by civil servants who were responsible to the Auditor-General for all public expenditure and who, for my own purposes, recorded my personal expenditure. Anyone of these officials could have produced a full and valid statement of how every penny was dealt with by the President's Office and exactly how my own salary was spent by me personally. If this had been done it would have been shown that I refused to accept, as a political gesture, any of the expense allowances allotted to the President by law. In the same way if my *Will* had been published in full it would have shown that I left nothing even to my own family but bequeathed everything I did possess to the Party and the State. Before the so-called enquiry none of these detailed accounts were produced. Yet Kojo Djaba was called to testify that I had in fact taken the money which he had been convicted of stealing.

The failure of the routine Police investigation of corruption made it necessary for me to deal with it either by setting up a special body as I did in Djaba's case or by appointing official Commissions of Enquiry to expose publicly notable members of our society and even Ministers of Government. Shortly before the army and police action on 24th February 1966, the Report of the Commission of Enquiry into Trade Malpractices in Ghana was published. It was a bold attempt to examine and to expose the activities of men and women who were sabotaging our economic development plans by indulging in various forms of trade malpractices. Some of our wealthiest and most prominent citizens were mentioned by name. There was an immediate demand that legal action should be taken against them, and this was under consideration when the military and police treachery took place.

Obviously this kind of exposure brought us new and powerful enemies. But these people, by acting in the way they did, were all the time secret enemies of the people, and it was essential to bring them to the surface.

I regard the events sparked off on 24th February 1966 as a cleansing process. All those who had for so long been working either openly or secretly against us came together and exposed themselves in their true colours for all to see. By their very actions, on 24th February and in the months of "N.L.C." rule, they have clearly shown themselves to be traitors to their country and the stooges of neo-colonialism. They have displayed their reactionary nature, their complete disregard for the common man and for the progress of the African Revolution.

It is like when you boil a pot hard; all the bits and pieces of useless stuff come to the top and you are able to skim them off easily. It is necessary to realise, that, in many ways, the so-called "coup d'état" has not been a set-back but has been merely a symptom of how neo-colonialism is breaking down.

Almost all African countries came to independence without armed struggle. This meant that it was impossible, in practice, to reconstruct these new states upon a socialist basis immediately. I was well aware of the compromises which it was necessary to make and the dangers which this entailed but Ghana's independence on any condition was the first essential in securing the freedom of Africa. Not to have seized independence when we had a chance of obtaining it, whatever the liability we inherited, would have been criminal. The circumstances under which the C.P.P. was formed resulted in it being a compromise organisation composed of some genuine revolutionaries but containing many of those who are interested in independence only so as to better themselves and to take the place of the previous colonial traders and businessmen. This meant that I had to include in any government which I formed representatives of all tendencies in the Party including businessmen on the make such as Emmanuel Ayeh-Kumi and William Halm. In the circumstances of the day there was at least a reasonable chance that such people would act honestly and would assist to build the state on a new basis.

The experiment which we tried in Ghana was essentially one of developing the country in co-operation with the world as a whole. Non-alignment meant exactly what it said. We were not hostile to the countries of the socialist world in the way in which the governments of the old colonial territories were. It should be remembered that while Britain pursued at home co-existence with the Soviet Union this was never allowed to extend to British colonial territories. Books on socialism, which were published and circulated freely in Britain, were banned in the British colonial empire, and after Ghana became independent it was assumed abroad that it would continue to follow the same restrictive ideological approach. When we behaved as did the British in their relations with the socialist countries we were accused of being pro-Russian and introducing the most dangerous ideas into Africa.

In fact, the fault was that, from the very circumstances in which we found ourselves, we were unable to introduce more "dangerous ideas" or to get them more widely understood. What went wrong in Ghana was not that we attempted to have friendly relations with the countries of the socialist world but that we maintained too friendly relations with the countries of the western bloc.

Before the military revolt the policy of Ghana was based upon an attempt to develop the country along what were essentially socialist lines. This policy could have succeeded had the western world been prepared to see coming into existence a genuinely independent African state. In fact, they were not prepared to do so and we thus gave innumerable hostages to fortune.

The "coup d'état" on its surface was a military revolt against myself and what I stood for. If it is analysed more deeply, however, it is a mark of the breakdown of the western attempt to influence and control Africa. The western countries, having failed to control democratically supported African governments, were forced into the final extremity of substituting regimes which depended upon no other mandate than the weapons which they held in their hands. Such puppet governments cannot survive for long either in Ghana or elsewhere in Africa. They are, in the first place, based on internal contradictions. Why they are tolerated is that their initial popularity is due to a sort of sympathetic magic. The prosperity of the western world at the moment depends upon exploiting less developed countries. Each year the western world pays less for its imports and each year charges more for its exports. Those who make our "coups" believe, however, or at least pretend to believe, that if they copy, or claim to copy, the outward image of the western world, then—in some miraculous way—they will secure the advantages which the

72

western world enjoys. The contrary is the case. The individuals who have made the counter-revolution from Saigon to Sierra Leone are dependent for their political existence upon western support. The countries over which they temporarily obtained control are therefore exploited all the more viciously. By supporting the reactionary rebellions in Africa the western countries have dug graves for imperialism and neo-colonialism and have put before the African people the clear choice which was unclear before, either to go forward with a thorough revolution or else to continue in a situation which, year by year, impoverishes and humiliates them further.

Events in Ghana since the military rebellion illustrate this admirably. Those who seized power claim they came forward to save the economy, restore prosperity, democracy, freedom of the press and the like. Instead, in order to maintain themselves in office at all they have had to impose harsher taxation, sell out state enterprises to foreign interests, murder democracy, curb the press and forcibly to suppress any type of consultation with the people. Instead, therefore, of proving that capitalism and the western way of life are the best, they demonstrate that it only brings increasing misery to all those who attempt to reproduce it in Africa. They thus, by their example, produce a genuinely revolutionary situation which did not previously exist and which was, through its absence, one of the main reasons for African disunity and for the poverty of the continent.

I had for long the gravest doubts about many of those in leading positions in my Party. Despite the establishment of the ideological institute at Winneba which I hoped might be used to teach some general understanding of what we were attempting it was clear to me that many in high positions still failed to understand the political and social purposes of the state. On Ghana's external policy, however, depended to a large extent the progressive line which Africa as a whole used to follow. I had to weigh against the desire to move fast at home the dangers of concentrating too much upon internal matters and achieving a revolution at home at the cost of temporarily withdrawing from the international field.

The conduct of many of those in the higher Party leadership has demonstrated to the people of Ghana that one can no longer trust in a broad coalition of interests. The old civil service and the Judiciary went over almost to a man to the usurping regime. By so doing they were of course serving personal interests and to this extent what they did was understandable if not excusable. The lesson, however, which their conduct provides, is that they had no loyalty to the state or understanding of the social purposes which we were attempting to achieve. It might be possible to work in the future with people who were merely dishonest through self-interest but it is absolutely impossible to utilize a machine which has shown itself so defective of understanding.

For these reasons, the "coup" has achieved something which it would have been impossible to achieve without it, namely, a complete and public exposure of the impossibility of continuing along old lines.

The slate has been wiped clean and now at least we can begin to build again upon new foundations. For the people of Ghana life under the "N.L.C." is a form of political education which they could never otherwise have had. For the C.P.P. it is an even more important lesson in that it shows that the old organisation was defective and that the old leadership in many cases which was inherited from the struggle against British imperialism was inadequate for its task and when put to the test of crisis failed.

In the old days popular opinion forced me to maintain in positions of authority individuals who were well-known in their localities through their local families and tribal influences. In the past many such people rendered important services to the Party. Now, however, a new testing time has arisen and these people, when weighed against events, have had all the defects of their characters exposed for the whole world to see.

In a larger sense the "coup d'état" has made it plain that the C.P.P. can no longer follow the path of the old line. It must develop a new and reformed revolutionary leadership which must come from the broad mass of the Party. There is now a genuinely revolutionary situation in Ghana. For this reason, while the present is dark, the future is bright. And indeed the misfortunes of Ghana in its darkest days are a necessary lesson for all African revolutionaries.

5

THE BIG LIE

It has been said that the fabrication of the "big lie" is essential in the planning of any usurpation of political power. In the case of Ghana, the big lie told to the world was that Ghana needed to be rescued from "economic chaos". Various other lies were hinged to this central lie. The country was said to be hopelessly in debt and the people on the verge of starvation. Among the lies aimed against me personally was the one that I had accumulated a large private fortune; this was to form the basis for an all-out character assassination attempt. But these lies were subsidiary to the one big lie of "economic mismanagement", which was to provide an umbrella excuse for the seizure of power by neo-colonialist inspired traitors.

If Ghana was in such a serious economic condition, why was there no lack of investment in her growing industries? Investors do not put their money into mismanaged enterprises and unstable economies. Why did the imperialist powers try to exert an economic squeeze on Ghana? No one in his right mind bothers to attack an already-dying concern. Who made up the figures of Ghana's supposed "debt"? Why was only one side of the ledger shown—why no mention of assets? How can the obvious evidence of the modernisation and industrialisation of Ghana, such as the new roads, factories, schools and hospitals, the harbour and town of Tema, the Volta and Teffle bridges and the Volta dam be reconciled with the charge of wasted expenditure? If the Ghanaian people were starving, why no evidence of this, and why no popular participation in the "coup"? How was it that Ghana had the highest living standard in Africa per capita, the highest literacy rate, and was the nearest to achieving genuine economic independence? All these questions, and many related to them, are now being asked. An examination of our development plans and of their implementation reveals the truth—that it was their success and not their failure which spurred our enemies into action. Ghana, on the threshold of economic independence, and in the vanguard of the African revolutionary struggle to achieve continental liberation and unity, was too dangerous an example to the rest of Africa to be allowed to continue under a socialist-directed government.

In the first ten years of its administration, the Ghana government drew up the First and Second Five Year Development Plans (1951-1956 and 1959-1964), and the Consolidation Plan, which covered the two-year gap between these Plans (1957-1959). Under these Plans the foundations were to be laid for the modernisation and industrialisation of Ghana. A skilled labour force was to be trained and an adequate complement of public services built up such as transport, electricity, water and telecommunications.

We had to work fast. Under colonial rule, foreign monopoly interests had tied up our whole economy to suit themselves. We had not a single industry. Our economy was dependent on one cash crop—cocoa. Although our output of cocoa is the largest in the world, there was not a single cocoa processing factory.

Before we took office in 1951 there was no direct railway between Accra and Takoradi, in those days our main port. Passengers and freight had to travel by way of Kumasi. This was because Kumasi was the centre of the timber and mining industries, both of which served foreign interests and were therefore well supplied with the necessary communications. There were few roads, and only a very rudimentary public transport system. For the most part, people walked from place to place. There were very few hospitals, schools or clinics. Most of our villages lacked a piped water supply. In fact, the nakedness of the land when my government began in 1951 has to have been experienced to be believed.

Failure to promote the interests of our people was due to the insatiable demands of colonial exploitation. It was not until we had grasped political power that we were in a position to challenge this, and to develop our resources for the benefit of the Ghanaian people. Those who would judge us merely by the heights we have achieved would do well to remember the depths from which we started.

The condition of Ghana in 1964 showed that our first two Development Plans had been carried out with a high degree of success. We had one of the most modern network of roads in Africa. Takoradi harbour had been extended, and the great artificial harbour at Tema, the largest in Africa, built from scratch. Large extensions to the supply of water and to the telecommunication network had been constructed, and further extensions were under construction. Our agriculture was being diversified and mechanised. Above all, the Volta River Project, which was designed to provide the electrical power for our great social, agricultural and industrialisation programme, was almost completed.

In education, progress was equally impressive. In ten years we had achieved more than in the whole period of colonial rule. The figures below show the great increase in the numbers of children in primary and middle schools, and of students in secondary and technical schools and in colleges of higher education.

	1951	1961	% Increase
Primary Schools	154,360	481,500	211.9
Middle Schools	66,175	160,000	141.7
Secondary and Technical Schools ...	3,559	19,143	437.8
Teacher Training Colleges ...	1,916	4,552	137.5
University Students	208	1,204	478.8

The building of schools and colleges was given top priority in our development plans. We took the unprecedented step in Africa of making all education free, from primary to university level. In addition, textbooks were supplied free to all pupils in primary, middle and secondary schools.

In the 1964-65 school year there were 9,988 primary and middle schools with an enrolment of 1,286,486. There were 89 secondary schools with 32,971 pupils; 47 teacher training colleges with an enrolment of 10,168; 11 technical schools and

3 universities. All this, in a population of 7,500,000 put Ghana in the lead among independent African states. At the same time, a mass literacy campaign has made Ghana the most literate country in the whole of Africa.

A look at some of the other social achievements during the Party's first ten years of office reveals a similar rate of progress.

BASIC SERVICES

	1951	1961	% Increase
Health			
Number of hospital beds ...	2,368	6,155	159.9
Rural and urban clinics	1	30	—
Doctors and dentists	156	500	220.5
Transport and Communications			
Roads (in miles)—			
Class I (Bitumen)	1,398	2,050	46.7
Class II (Gravel)	2,093	3,346	59.8
(Since 1961 the mileage of motor roads has risen to 19,236. Feeder roads connect most villages to the trunk road network.)			
Post Offices	444	779	75.4
Telephones	7,383	25,488	245.2
Electricity			
Installed electrical capacity (kW)	84,708	120,860	42.7
Electrical power generated (kW '000)	281,983	390,174	38.4

In 1962 the government adopted what was known as the Party's Programme of Work and Happiness. It proclaimed our fundamental objective as the building of a socialist state devoted to the welfare of the masses.

The concrete programme of action for this was worked out in the Seven Year Development Plan launched on 11th March 1964. In presenting the Plan to the National Assembly I said that its main tasks were first, to speed up the rate of growth of our national economy; secondly, to enable us to embark upon the socialist transformation of our economy through the rapid development of the state and co-operative sectors; thirdly, to eradicate completely the colonial structure of our economy.

The Plan embodied measures aimed to achieve a self-sustaining economy founded on socialist production and distribution—an economy balanced between agriculture and industry, providing sufficient food for the people and supporting secondary industries based on the products of our agriculture. Ghana was to be as soon as possible a socialist state. The people, through the state, would have an effective share in the economy of the country and an effective control over it. Thus the principles of scientific socialism would be applied to suit our own particular situation.

The Party has always proclaimed socialism as its objective. But socialism cannot be achieved without socialists, much hard work and sacrifice, and detailed economic planning to provide a vast improvement in the level of material wealth of the country, and distribution of this wealth among the population. It was decided in the Seven Year Plan that Ghana's economy would for the time being remain a mixed one, with a vigorous public and co-operative sector operating alongside the private sector. Our socialist objectives demanded, however, that the public and co-operative sectors should expand faster than the private sector, especially those strategic areas of production upon which the economy of the country essentially depended.

Various state corporations and enterprises were to be established as a means of securing our economic independence and assisting in the national control of the economy. They were, like all business undertakings, expected to maintain themselves efficiently, and to show profits which could be used for further investment and to help finance public services. A State Management Committee was set up to ensure their efficient and profitable management.

Many state enterprises were quick to show results. The Ghana National Trading Corporation (G.N.T.C.) made a net profit of £4,885,900 in 1965, and had become the largest trading concern in the country. Other state enterprises, by their very nature, took a longer time to develop, and by February 1966 were only just beginning to make a profit. A few, notably in the agricultural sector, were in their infancy and were not expected to yield significant results for some time to come. A certain period of adaptation is necessary for all young industries, particularly in developing countries where the patterns of production are still mainly agricultural and elementary.

But it is noteworthy that the traitors of February 1966 found no less than 63 state enterprises which they could put on the market.

In our Seven Year Plan we recognised the value of foreign investment in the private sector, particularly in the production of consumer goods, the local processing of Ghanaian raw materials and the utilisation of Ghana's natural resources in the areas of economic activity where a large volume of investment was required. But we welcomed foreign investors in a spirit of partnership. We did not intend to allow them to operate in such a way as to exploit our people. They were to assist in the expansion of our economy in line with our general objectives, an agreed portion of their profits being allocated to promote the welfare and happiness of the Ghanaian people.

The state retained control of the strategic branches of the economy, including public utilities, raw materials, and heavy industry. The state also participated in light and consumer goods industries in which the rates of return on capital were highest. We intended that those industries which provided the basic living needs of the people should be state-owned in order to prevent any exploitation.

It was estimated that during the seven years there would be a total expenditure of £1,016 million. Total government investment in the Plan was to be £476 million. Foreign investors, individual Ghanaians, local authorities and the co-operative sector were expected to invest about £440 million. Ghanaians, it was hoped, would contribute nearly £100 million of direct labour in the construction of buildings, in community development and in the extension of their farms.

Special attention was given to the modernising of agriculture, so that a greater yield and a diversity of crops could be produced. We needed to produce more food locally so that we could reduce our imports of foodstuffs and at the same time improve the health of the people by increasing the protein content in the average diet. Most developing countries face nutritional problems of one kind or another. In our case, the great need was for more fish and meat to provide a properly balanced diet. We planned to increase the output of fish from an estimated 70,000 tons in 1963 to 250,000 tons in 1969. Livestock production, including poultry and eggs, was to increase from 20,080 tons to 37,800 tons.

Immediate steps were taken to expand the fishing fleet and to develop fish processing and marketing facilities. We bought 29 fishing trawlers from Russia. The immense man-made lake formed as part of the Volta River Project was being stocked with fish, and this too was about to bring a big improvement in the diet of the Ghanaian people.

As for meat and poultry, the government subsidised the development of many poultry farms, and the rearing of large herds of cattle. In colonial days, fresh meat, milk and eggs were available to Europeans only. Before the setback of February 1966, however, they were becoming part of the regular diet of the Ghanaian masses.

The task of correcting the imbalance in our food economy was regarded as the greatest challenge to the agricultural sector of the Plan. Far-reaching schemes were initiated for major improvements in irrigation and water conservation in the Northern and Upper Regions of Ghana. Peasant farmers throughout the country were informed that they would be able to make use of the agricultural machinery of state and co-operative farms. It was not the government's intention to squeeze out the peasant farmer. Far from it, we needed the maximum effort of every individual farmer if we were to achieve our agricultural targets.

During the period of the Plan, Ghana's production of raw materials was to be considerably increased. Cocoa, our main export, earned the country 1,680 million cedis between 1951 and 1961. Of this, the farmers received 1,008 million cedis and the remainder was used by the government and the Cocoa Marketing Board for maintaining public services and for the general development of the country. We increased our cocoa production from 264,000 tons in 1956-57, to 590,000 tons in 1963-64, and huge silos had been built, able to store half the cocoa crop, to enable us to restrict exports and so ensure a fair price for our cocoa in the world market.

Plans were also far advanced to increase exports of timber, and to develop new species of wood for buildings, furniture and other wood products, and for use in paper factories. Efforts were being made to revive our once-flourishing export crop of palm oil. Rubber production was being increased. In the Western Region, a vast new plantation, 18 miles long, had been sown.Within two to three years Ghana was to be one of the greatest rubber producers in Africa. The production of palm oil, cotton, sugar cane and tobacco was being stepped up. By 1970, there were to be four factories in operation producing 100,000 tons of sugar a year, more than sufficient to eliminate the item from our list of imports.

Greatest of all our development projects was the Volta dam. When the Seven Year Plan was launched, the Volta Project was expected to begin to generate electrical power by September 1965. Completion of the Project would enable us to develop the full industrial potential of Ghana. It would increase by nearly 600 per cent the installed electrical capacity of the country. Nearly one-half of this new capacity would be taken up by the aluminium smelter in Tema; it is estimated that Ghana has sufficient bauxite to last for 200 years. But apart from this the Volta Project would have an ample reserve of power for other users, and Ghana would have liberated herself decisively from the possibility of a power shortage becoming a brake on the rate of economic progress.

Construction targets for the various parts of the Volta River Project were achieved, some of them ahead of schedule, and the official inauguration ceremony took place on 23rd January 1966. At that time, building was about to start on a large subsidiary dam at Bui. Plans were also well advanced for the construction of an alumina plant which would have given Ghanaians control of the whole process of aluminium production. As it was, we were exporting bauxite to the United Kingdom for processing while we were importing alumina manufactured in the United States from bauxite mined in Jamaica for our aluminium smelter.

In keeping with my government's policy of linking Ghana's progress with Africa's total development, provision was made in the Plan for economic co-operation with other African states. As I said in my address to the National Assembly on 11th March 1964:

> "While we wait for the setting up of a Union Government for Africa, we must begin immediately to harmonise our plans for Africa's total development. For example, I see no reason why the independent African states should not, with advantage to each other, join together in an economic union and draw up together a

joint Development Plan which will give us greater scope and flexibility to our mutual advantage. By the same token, I see no reason why the independent African states should not have common shipping and air lines in the interests of improved services and economy. With such rationalisation of our economic policies, we could have common objectives and thus eliminate unnecessary competition and frontier barriers and disputes."

When in fact I inaugurated the completed Volta River Project on 23rd January 1966, I said: "We are ready and prepared to supply power to our neighbours in Togo, Dahomey, Ivory Coast and Upper Volta. As far as I am concerned this project is not for Ghana alone. Indeed, I have already offered to share our power resources with our sister African states."

On that day at Akosombo, some 60 miles north-east of Accra, when I switched on illuminating lights signifying the official opening of hydro-electric power from the Volta, one of my greatest dreams had come true. I had witnessed the wide-scale electrification of Ghana and the breakthrough into a new era of economic and social advance. The Volta Dam permitted not only a large aluminium plant at Tema processing the country's rich bauxite deposits, but a broad range of other industrial projects. The initial power output is 512,000 kW (588,000 kW at full load) and the ultimate power output will be 768,000 kW (882,000 kW at full load). There are 500 miles of transmission lines. The main grid carries 161,000 volts.

The water building up behind the dam is forming the largest man-made lake in the world. It will cover an area of 3,275 square miles with a capacity of 120 million acre feet of water, and will be 250 miles long, with a shore-line of 4,500 miles. Approximately 80,000 people had to be moved from the area submerged by the lake. This necessitated the construction of 50 new villages and towns to accommodate them, the provision of modern housing, schools, piped water, electricity, medical facilities and new forms of employment. Thousands of acres of land had to be cleared, and people settled on farms and smallholdings with up-to-date methods of cultivation and animal husbandry. All this was achieved.

The creation of the Volta Lake has already provided facilities for an important fresh-water fishing industry. The Volta

River contained numerous excellent indigenous fish; and research has shown which fish to breed to increase the supply, and how to control weed growth. A number of ports and fishing villages being formed round the lake-side provide bases for a cheap means of transport from the north to the south of Ghana. Furthermore, the lake forms a vast reservoir, making possible the improvement of water supplies to towns and villages and the irrigation of land for agriculture. The natural seasonal fluctuation in the level of the lake will immediately affect 650 square miles of land, permitting the cultivation of rice and other crops. Lake Volta was also to be developed as a holiday and tourist attraction.

Ghanaians are justifiably proud that their own government provided £35,000,000, that is half of the cost of the Volta River Project as well as meeting the cost of the new port and township of Tema, which was an essential part of the scheme. The balance of the £70,000,000 required was to be raised by international loans as follows:

International Bank for Reconstruction and Development	£16,790,000
Agency for International Development of the United States Government ...	£9,640,000
Export-Import Bank of the United Kingdom Government	£3,570,000
United Kingdom Board of Trade acting for the Export Credits Guarantee Department	£5,000,000

Incidentally, at a time when our detractors talk much of bribery and corruption in the developing countries, it is noteworthy that not a single penny went astray or was misappropriated in the entire Volta undertaking, which involved countless contracts over many years.

Apart from completing the Volta River Project, the Seven Year Development Plan provided for certain further improvements in the physical services. These were mostly intended to improve upon the existing system of transport, communications, water supply and electricity services in order to make them fully capable of supporting the proposed level of industrial and agricultural development.

A considerable proportion of the increase in material wealth that was expected to accrue to the country during the seven years of the Plan's operation was to be used to promote public welfare services. Education, the health services and housing were all to benefit. As far as health services were concerned, the Plan proposed to change the main orientation which had hitherto been more curative than preventative. Rural health services were developed in such a way that the rate of infant mortality was lowered, and maternity and post-natal care improved. The main cause of poor health in Ghana is the prevalence of endemic diseases such as malaria. The Plan put emphasis on the fight against these endemic diseases.

New regional hospitals, equipped with all specialist facilities, were under construction in Tamale, Koforidua, Ho and Sunyani, and existing hospitals were being improved. Arrangements had been made to build six new district hospitals and four more urban polyclinics to assist in the decentralisation of out-patient work. In addition, five new mental hospitals with accommodation for 1,200 patients were designed to be ready by 1970. They were to be backed up by psychiatric units providing treatment for as many mental patients as possible.

The urgent need for more doctors was being met by sending Ghanaian medical students to study abroad, and by the setting up of our own medical school. In 1962, 51 pre-medical students were enrolled at the University of Ghana. When our own medical school is functioning fully it will be empowered to provide a screening system for all doctors trained abroad who wish to practise in Ghana. The medical programme under the Seven Year Development Plan was intended to achieve the following ratios:

1 doctor to 10,000 people
1 nurse to 5,000 patients (including patients in public health centres)
1 technician (laboratory, X-ray, etc.) to 5,000 patients
1 health inspector to 15,000 people
1 health auxiliary (vaccinators, dressing-room attendants, etc.) to 1,000 people.

A large network of health centres was being built all over Ghana to serve the rural population, and regional health officers were being provided with training and facilities to enable them to carry out their important work.

The only nursing school which existed in 1945 produced only 8 nurses a year by 1950. In 1961-62 six schools of nursing turned out 265 new nurses and midwives.

Perhaps the most outstanding contribution to public health has come from the Medical Field Unit. This unit was formed to seek out and control trypanosomiasis, and it has been successful in containing the disease. It has also carried out a massive vaccination programme, and played a leading role in the control of epidemics of cerebrospinal meningitis. It is currently actively engaged in combating malaria, leprosy and tuberculosis.

In launching the Seven Year Development Plan, with all its detailed programmes for our country's economic and social progress, I warned about the existence of Ghanaian private enterprise in our midst. It was necessary, I told members of the National Assembly, to distinguish between the two types of business which had grown up within recent years. The first was the type which it was the government's intention to encourage, that of the small businessman who employed his capital in an industry or trade with which he was familiar, and which fulfilled a public need. The second consisted of that class of Ghanaian businesses which were modelled on the old colonial pattern of exploitation. In this category were those who used their capital, not in productive endeavour, but to purchase and resell, at high prices, commodities such as salt, fish and other items of food and consumer goods which were in demand by the people. This type of business served no social purpose, and steps would be taken to see that the nation's banking resources were not used to provide credit for them.

Even more harmful to the economy was another type of enterprise in which some Ghanaians had been participating. This was the setting up of bogus agencies for foreign companies which were in fact nothing more than organisations for distributing bribes and for exerting improper pressures on behalf of foreign companies. The government intended to carry out a thorough investigation into the activities of these agencies and to suppress them.

The initiative of Ghanaian businessmen would not be cramped, but we intended to take steps to see that is was channelled towards desirable social ends and was not expended in the exploitation of the community. We would discourage any-thing which threatened our socialist objectives. For this reason, no Ghanaian would be allowed to take up shares in any enter-prise under foreign investment. Instead, our people would be encouraged to save by investing in the state sector and in co-operative undertakings.

This, in essence, was our Seven Year Development Plan, a Plan scientifically worked out with the participation of some of the world's leading experts on economic and social plan-ning. It was to integrate educational, industrial and agricul-tural programmes to bring full employment and to make possible the achievement of economic independence and a big rise in our living standards. And this was the Plan the rebel military regime scrapped as soon as it usurped power.

No possible justification can be given for its abandonment and the sell-out of Ghana's increasing assets. The first phase of the Plan was going well, and according to schedule. During the first year, £48,900,000 was spent on development projects, and of this amount, £16 million went into the key sectors, agriculture and industry. In agriculture, the emphasis was on diversification. State farms cultivated 24,000 acres of rubber, oil palm, banana, urena, lobata, coconut and citrus. Together with the agricultural wing of the Workers Brigade, which alone had 12,500 acres, the two institutions cultivated large areas for cereals and vegetables. During this period also, improvements were made in the modernisation and productivity of private and co-operative farms.

In the industrial sphere, during this period, nearly all the initiative was in the public sector. The construction of many new industrial plants were undertaken. These included a steel-works (30,000 tons), two cocoa processing plants, one at Takoradi (28,000 tons) and the other at Tema (68,600 tons), two sugar refineries, a textile printing plant, a glass factory, a chocolate factory, a meat processing plant, a radio assembly plant and a large printing works at Tema. All these factories were brought into production during the first phase of the Plan.

In addition, work was well advanced on a textile mill and a complex of food industries at Tema, a gold refinery at Tarkwa, and asbestos, cement, shoe and rubber-tyre factories

87

at Kumasi. The buildings for an atomic reactor at Kwabinya were almost finished. So also was a plant for the manufacture of pre-fabricated houses. In fact, the basic policy underlying the Seven Year Development Plan, to change the structure of our mainly agricultural economy into a balanced modern economy, was going ahead with great speed and efficiency. We were successfully managing to use our local raw materials for establishing industries, and were beginning to satisfy local demand for certain consumer goods. For example, we produced matches, shoes, nails, sweets, chocolate, soft drinks, whisky, beer, gin, etc., cigarettes, biscuits, paints, canned fruit, insecticides and other chemicals. An indication of the build-up of our industrial strength may be seen in the fact that at the beginning of January 1966 imports of raw materials amounted to about 9 per cent of Ghana's total imports.

Before the February action, the government was investing £25 million annually in manufacturing projects, and the country's main exports:

Cocoa	...	...	680	million cedis annually
Timber	...	...	31.2	„ „ „
Minerals		...	48	„ „ „

were providing a sound basis for profitable industrial enterprise.

On an average, Ghana annually imports about 264 million cedis of semi-finished and finished products consisting mainly of food and drinks, textiles and clothing, construction materials and capital equipment. Annual exports average some 254.4 million cedis of primary produce, mainly cocoa, timber, gold, diamonds and manganese. Our growing industries were to make possible a cut in imports, particularly of consumer goods, and an increase in our exports, not only of primary produce but of our own locally-manufactured products.

A look at the orientation of Ghana's investment policy during recent years throws further light on the direction in which Ghana was moving. In 1951-1959 90 per cent (i.e. £127.8 million) of government expenditure was allocated to provide social services and to create the infrastructure of economic growth, while 10 per cent (£13.4 million) went to the productive sector. During the 1951-1962 period, an average amount of £15.5 million was allocated yearly to the public sector during the First Development Plan, and during the Consolidated Plan an average of £21.4 million yearly. Under the Second Development Plan an average amount of £50 million yearly went to the public sector. Under the Seven Year Development Plan an average of £68 million was going to the public sector yearly, representing a total investment of £442 million for development projects belonging to the public sector. To the above-mentioned £68 million, £34 million were added for the Volta complex—in all £476 million for the public sector.

Investments during the Seven Year Development Plan period (1964-1970) were therefore distributed between social services and infrastructure (62%) and the directly productive sector (38%). This represented for Ghanaians an investment of £10 per head, per year (to be compared with the maximum investment of 8 shillings per head, per year, in countries associated with the Common Market during the 1958-1962 period). It may also be noted that Ghana has a 240 cedis per capita income, that is to say, practically the highest in independent Africa—and in real terms, the highest in Africa, since it cannot be considered that the distribution of gross national product is equitable in countries like South Africa, Rhodesia and most of the neo-colonialist states.

The qualitative aspect of Ghana's imports reveals that while consumer goods dropped from one-half of total imports in 1961 to two-fifths in 1963, industrial equipment and goods increased from 50.6 per cent of total imports in 1961 to 60.6 per cent in 1963.

On the question of ownership, it is worth noting that in 1965 the state controlled between 60 per cent and 65 per cent of the national production (this percentage was to rise in 1970), and that since 1963, the total gold and foreign exchange assets of Ghana, and total capital exports, were likewise under state financial control.

Apart from a 41 per cent control over consumer goods imports, the state was controlling in 1965 over 60 per cent of the exports in the most important sectors such as gold, diamonds, cocoa. In the case of timber, the Timber Marketing Board had increased its foreign exchange earnings from £5.7 million in 1962 to £8 million in 1964, and was able during the same period, to grant revolving loans of £2 million to Ghanaian producers organised into co-operatives.

When the Party came to power in 1951, all imported goods were in the hands of a few big foreign firms, especially the monopolist United Africa Company, part of the Unilever complex. Foreign firms dominated Ghana's trade and virtually controlled the economy. By 1965, however, the grip was being broken. The nationalised Ghana National Trading Corporation was distributing 32 per cent of all imports.

My government was also breaking through the stranglehold of the big international banking houses. In 1958, foreign banks held one-third of Ghana's foreign currency reserves; in 1965 they held none.

Our success in breaking the web of economic control which Western capitalism has imposed across the whole of the African continent, and our clear socialist policies, provoked the hostility of the imperialist powers. They knew that as long as I was alive and at the head of the Party in Ghana the process could not be halted and neo-colonialist exploitation could not be re-imposed. Ours was a system they could neither penetrate nor manipulate.

Significantly, one of the first acts of the "N.L.C." was to announce the abandonment of the Seven Year Development Plan, which would have given the Ghanaian people the only worthwhile independence—real economic independence. The "N.L.C." replaced it with a two-year "review period" during which the socialised industries would be dismantled and the door opened once more to unrestricted "private enterprise"—in fact, they were establishing a neo-colonialist economic subjugation of Ghana.

The only Ghanaians to benefit from such a sell-out were the African middle-class hangers-on to neo-colonialist privilege and the neo-colonialist trading firms. For the mass of workers, peasants and farmers, the victims of the capitalist free-for-all, it meant a return to the position of "drawers of water and hewers of wood" to Western capitalism.

Of course, the Ghanaian economy was not without its problems, but is this not true of all national economies, and particularly those of developing countries in the context of the growing gap between rich and poor nations? In any event, these difficulties were not determinant. It was no mean achieve·ment that in January 1965, after five years as a Republic, Ghana had 63 state enterprises and a budget of £200 million, including a supplementary budget, for its population of nearly eight million; while Nigeria, richer in national resources and with a population of 55 million, had a budget of £78 million.

Imperialist circles have talked much about Ghana's external debt, given as £250 million. Apart from the dubious accounting which arrived at this conveniently round sum, a figure such as this means nothing unless it is set in the context of the overall Ghanaian economic situation. To implement our various Development Plans it was necessary to borrow considerable sums of money, but it was borrowed on the basis of building capital assets such as the Volta dam, and over 100 industries established in Ghana since independence. The government made sure that the international agreements signed were based on economic feasibility, and that the money borrowed could create something lasting and beneficial not only for us in our lifetime but for the generations to follow. Seen in the light of Ghana's growing industries and increasing exports, her "indebtedness" is put in proper perspective—as an index of the investors' confidence in the enterprise and the management they helped to finance. In addition, it should be noted that only some £20 million was due to be paid in 1967, and this did not prevent the government from refusing the political conditions attached to a loan from the International Monetary Fund (I.M.F.).

Long faces are pulled at the drop in our foreign reserves since independence. In 1957, Ghana had a sterling balance of £200 million. This has not been "squandered" as the imperialist press would have its readers believe. It has been used to pay off succcessive balance of payments deficits due to the rise in prices of imported consumer goods, and the drastic fall in the price of our main export crop—cocoa. It should be remembered that the sterling balance was in fact a forced loan at negligible interest which Britain acquired from Ghana during and after the Second World War. Its accumulation was made possible by the Cocoa Marketing Board which prevented Ghanaian cocoa growers from receiving the bulk of the proceeds from the sale of their cocoa. The capital the growers might have amassed from cocoa profits and later might have invested in industry was locked up in London "to maintain the confidence of the foreign investor".

Our imperialist critics would be better employed examining the economic situation in their own countries, many of which are in grave financial difficulties. In Britain, for example, the £1 is devalued, there is a continuous "balance of payments crisis" and unemployment is a serious problem.

In Ghana, before 24th February 1966, unemployment was virtually unknown. All salaries were regularly paid and new jobs were constantly being created as the Seven Year Development Plan was being implemented. It was estimated that more than one million new workers would be needed to fill the new jobs which would be created, and also to replace those who left the labour force during the Plan period. More than 500,000 of them would be employed in industry and agriculture, and another 400,000 would be needed in government services, commerce and construction. The remainder were to be employed in transport, mining and the public utility services. In fact, plans were being made to import labour.

When neo-colonialist inspired traitors seized power in February 1966, we were expanding our educational system to provide the necessary numbers of qualified people to meet these new demands. Changes were made to shorten and to improve educational courses. For example, there was a reduction made in the number of school years so that University graduates would be ready for employment at the age of 21 or 22 instead of 24 or 25 as used to be the case. Under the new plan, the time spent in middle school was reduced by two years and the secondary school period by one year. Primary education took six years and was followed by two years of vocationally oriented training for those who did not intend to proceed to secondary schools. The reduction by two years of the ten-year middle school programme was designed to permit 300,000 additional young people to join the labour force during the seven-year period, and to equip them with basic training in technical and agricultural skills.

The figures below illustrate the planned growth in school enrolment 1963-1970:

92

	Total enrolment	
	1963	1970
Primary—Middle ...	1,200,000	2,200,000
Secondary	23,000	78,000
Teacher Training ...	6,000	21,000
Technical Schools ...	4,000	6,000
Clerical Training ...	100	5,000
Universities	2,000	5,000

The intake would be such that from 1968 nearly 250,000 children would complete primary-middle school and 20,000 others would leave secondary school each year. For the entire Plan period, the output from all educational institutions was to have been approximately as follows:

Middle and continuing schools ...	750,000
Secondary schools	46,000
Universities	9,000
Technical schools	14,000
Secretarial schools	11,000
Teacher training	31,000

The tremendous rate of our educational growth created certain difficulties. We needed many more trained teachers, and more school and college buildings. We were successfully overcoming these problems. The government allocated 153.6 million cedis (£64 million) for the construction of post-primary school buildings to feed the new secondary and higher educational institutions. The University of Ghana, the Kwame Nkrumah University of Science and Technology, and Cape Coast University College were supplying a large number of teachers; and expatriate teachers had been recruited to fill other vacancies until our own output of teachers was sufficient to cope with the demand. The Cape Coast University College was to have become a fully-fledged University in September 1966, but the "N.L.C." has abandoned the plan.

Local authorities and individual communities were primarily responsible for the provision of elementary school facilities, though the government provided teachers, textbooks and other services for primary schools. Special subsidies were given to less favoured parts of the country to help in the development of primary education.

To assist in solving the manpower problem, the Trades

Union Congress, the Ministry of Labour and employers' associations launched and rapidly expanded in-service training schemes to augment the knowledge and technical skill of all new employees. Adult education facilities were also being improved to provide part-time and evening classes for craftsmen, foremen, technicians and managers. The Institute of Public Education, the Workers' College, the Universities and other specialised institutions were redoubling their efforts to make this type of education available throughout the country.

Ghana was going ahead. The nation's economy was almost completely controlled by Ghanaians, and our educational planning was producing educated and skilled personnel to meet the demand. Likewise, thorough-going machinery had been established for the political education of the masses so that our socialist objectives, and Ghana's role in the wider African revolution, might be clearly understood. This was the purpose of the Young Pioneers, the T.U.C. educational programme, and the Ideological Institute of Winneba where cadres were being trained. It was to make possible the unfolding of the next phase of the Ghanaian revolution: the establishment of a socialist republic, the principle of which was enshrined in the 1961 Constitution of the Republic of Ghana.

This process was well on its way when in 1965, the imperialists and neo-colonialists stepped up their pressure on Ghana in the form of an economic squeeze. In that year, the price of cocoa on the world market was artificially forced down from £476 in 1954 to £87 10s. a ton (1965). This meant that although Ghana exported 500,000 tons of cocoa, she earned only £77 million, or less than her receipts in the mid-1950's for 250,000 tons.

When the Seven Year Development Plan was drawn up, it was assumed that the price of cocoa on the world market would be at least £200 a ton. This was not an unreasonable assumption. Between 1953 and 1963, prices fell only once below £190 a ton. In 1954 the price was £476, and in 1957-58 it was £352. But the very year the Seven Year Development Plan was launched, cocoa prices began to fall steeply. At the same time, the prices of capital and manufactured goods needed for industrial and agricultural projects under the Plan were rapidly rising. Between 1950 and 1961 they had risen by over 25 per cent.

94

In 1964, the imperialist powers, the principal consumers of cocoa, promised at the Geneva meeting of the United Nations Conference on Trade and Development (U.N-C.T.A.D.) that they would "lift barriers in the form of tariffs and duties on primary products, either raw, processed or semi-processed". This would have meant that cocoa-grindings, cocoa butter and chocolate products whose price was firm, could have been sold in the metropolitan markets to cushion the effects of the low cocoa prices. But Britain and the U.S.A. did not keep their promise to lower trade barriers against processed and semi-processed primary products. Ghana, regarded by them as a pace-setter in Africa, could not be allowed to succeed in build-ing socialism.

When I spoke to the Ghana cocoa farmers on 22nd September 1965, I drew attention to the breach of faith of the cocoa consumers and said that if tariff walls prevented us from sell-ing our chocolate abroad we could still sell it in Ghana and in other African countries at a price well within the means of all. I announced that cocoa powder was being distributed to schoolchildren, and that the production of cocoa butter, in demand for the manufacture of cosmetics and pharmaceuti-cals, was being expanded.

We constructed silos which, when completed, would enable us to withhold more than half of our cocoa crop from the world market. This amount would be more than the combined world cocoa surplus of production over consumption. We were, in fact, breaking through the cocoa price squeeze. The U.S.A., however, was stockpiling a record quantity of cocoa to be used to keep prices down. In its 1966 Commodity Review, the United Nations Food and Agricultural Organisation (F.A.O.), reported that the total stocks of cocoa beans in con-suming countries at the end of 1964 amounted to 500,000 tons, and that by December 1965 this total was further increased.

The U.S.A. and Britain could, if they had wanted, have fixed a reasonable price for cocoa and so have eased the economic situation in Ghana. They had no wish to do so. On the contrary, the forcing down of the price of cocoa was part of their policy of preparing the economic ground for political action in the form of a "coup" and a change of government.

Throughout 1965, and before then, the U.S. government exerted various other forms of economic pressure on Ghana.

It withheld investment and credit guarantees from potential investors, put pressure on existing providers of credit to the Ghanaian economy, and negated applications for loans made by Ghana to American-dominated financial institutions such as the I.M.F.

This pressure ended smartly after 24th February 1966 when the U.S. State Department's political objective had been achieved. The price of cocoa suddenly rose on the world market, and the I.M.F. rushed to the aid of the "N.L.C."

If further proof were needed of America's political motives it may be seen in the U.S. government's hysterical reaction to the publication of my book, *Neo-Colonialism — The Last Stage of Imperialism* in October 1965. In this book I exposed the economic stranglehold exercised by foreign monopolistic complexes such as the Anglo-American Corporation, and illustrated the ways in which this financial grip perpetuated the paradox of Africa: poverty in the midst of plenty. The American Government sent me a note of protest, and promptly refused Ghana $35 million of "aid".

The fact that our enemies decided finally on subversion and violence as the only effective way in which to achieve their objective of halting the Ghanaian revolution and bringing Ghana into the neo-colonialist fold, is a measure of the success of our economic policies. We had proved that we were strong enough to develop independently, not only without foreign tutelage, but also in the context of active imperialist and neo-colonialist resistance.

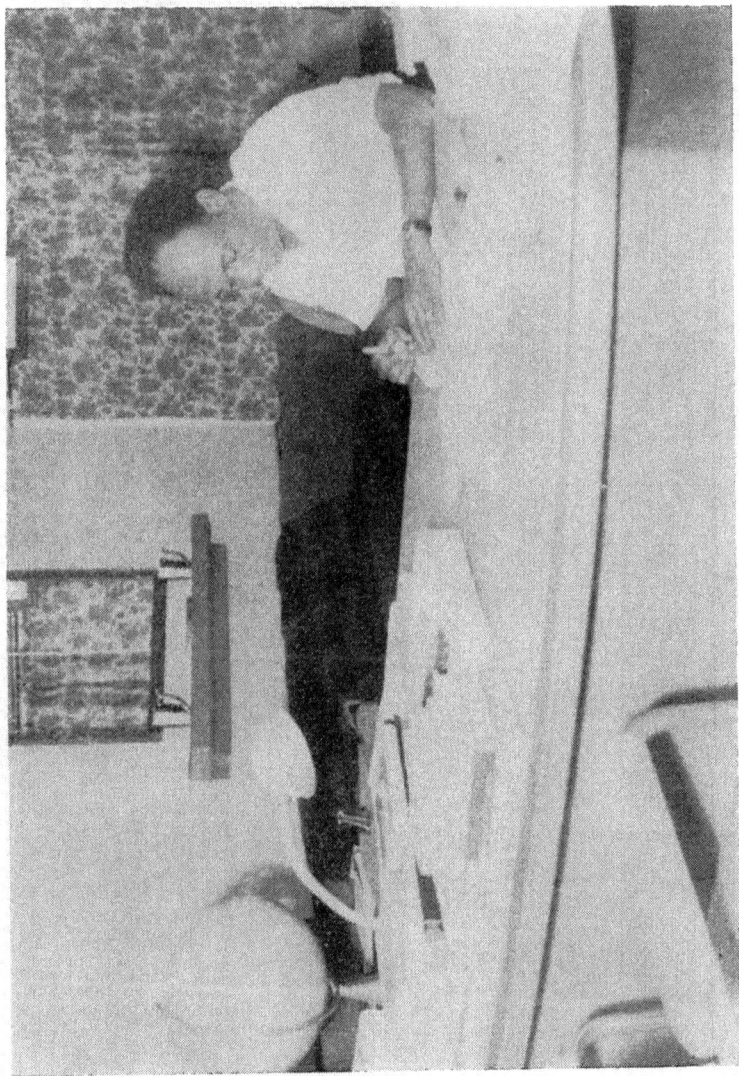

At my desk, Villa Syli.

Conakry, 1966

Among my roses, Villa Syli.

Conakry, 1967

On the terrace, Villa Syli.

Conakry, 1968

Front Row, left to right: E. K. Amponsah, S. Amoyawo, I. N. Adjekum, M. ⸻
Williams, Jnr., M. E. Appoh, Adayi Quarm, L. K. Eshun, F. A. Adia⸻
A. Yankey, Jnr., Leo Blay, K. Abaidoo, E. K. Tumi.
2nd Row: George Bartels, B. Andam, S. E. Cobbinah, E. E. Ediem, A. Q. Codjo⸻
J. K. Kosi, A. Yankey, Snr., A K. Buah, M. A. Mensah, S. Amoako-Att⸻
J. B. Quarshie, B. E. Quarm, Sam Baidoe, J. K. Armah.
3rd Row: J. K. Darmoe, N. K. Lartey, J. E. Appiah, James Buabeng, E. ⸻
Ofusu, P. K. Wansimah, Harry Ketibuah, Ambrose Akorsey, J. K. Ackc⸻
J. N. Attobrah, O. A. A. Sowah, I. Y. Anaman, Daniel Kweku, S. K. Sacke⸻
G. K. Adane, I. K. Buah, R. Y. Affum, E. A. Ayaim.

Members of my entourag⸻

4th Row: I. S. Essuman, E. Q. Lamptey, A. C. K. Amoabeng, Ben Famiyeh, S. K. Ibrahim, A. C. K. Baah, E. K. Baah, E. Kloutse, P. A. Quaicoe, E. K. Sackey, M. A. Cobbold, S. K. Koomson, F. K. Amoah, P. K. Amoah, R. F. Eduku, Emmanuel Obeng.
5th Row: I. K. Buah, J. K. Mensah, P. K. Amoo, David Ghartey, E. R. Amoah, Fred Oppong, J. B. Mensah, W. Sarfo, N. Nyamikeh, J. K. A. Sedziafa, J. K. Etse, J. Ohene, T. A. Lanquaye, M. K. Assuah.
6th Row: F. K. Abekah, A. Y. Kwofie, Bannerman-Smith, B. K. Forjoe, S. B. Boateng.

accompanied me to Guinea.

March, 1966

With President and Madame Sékou Touré.

Conakry, 1967

In the stadium.

With President Sékou Touré and his son.

6

SET BACK

The counter-revolutionary nature of the military-police regime in Ghana became obvious within hours of its establishment. Steps were taken immediately by the "N.L.C." to destroy our socialist gains and achievements, and to end Ghana's active participation in the African Revolution. In other words, we were to witness the all too familiar pattern and techniques of an imperialist and neo-colonialist attack, through a puppet government, on both socialism and the African continental struggle for liberation and unity.

One of the first acts of the "N.L.C." was to announce the abandonment of the Seven Year Development Plan. Work was stopped on state enterprises and industries and they were offered for sale to private investors. Ghana was thrown wide open, as in colonial days, to all the foreign exploitation we had worked so hard to end. The imperialist press, reflecting the jubilation in government circles in Washington, London, Bonn, Salisbury and Johannesburg, displayed such headings as: "Ghana Swings to the West," "The New Ghana Moves Westwards," and "Ghana Comes to Heel." Ghana was being sold into political and economic slavery. Her image in Africa and the world was being destroyed and the drive towards an All-African Union Government set back.

It is significant that Major-General Sir Edward Spears, Chairman of Ashanti Goldfields, was among the first to congratulate the military and police traitors. He had accepted the hospitality of my government for the inauguration of the Volta River Project and was still in Ghana when the action took place. He at once sent a message to the "N.L.C.," requesting an interview "at 7 p.m. on Thursday, March 3rd". He was immediately given the appointment he had asked for. Spears must have been very sure of his ground. It is hardly customary for businessmen to name the precise time and date of a meeting with heads of government. But as Spears said in his report to the shareholders of the Ashanti Goldfields Corporation on 30th March 1966: "Before I had my talk with General Ankrah, there were already indications that we would find the new regime much more satisfactory to deal with than the old." As puppets of neo-colonialists, members of the "N.L.C." were right from the start committed to an economic sell-out.

Businessmen from the U.S.A., from Britain, West Germany, Israel and elsewhere, flew into Ghana like vultures to grab the richest pickings. Virtually all the state-owned industries developed by my government were allowed to pass into private ownership. These included such enterprises as The Timber Products Corporation, The Cocoa Products Corporation, the Diamond Mining Corporation, the National Steel Works, the Black Star Shipping Line, Ghana Airways, and all the state-owned hotels.

As a result of the economic sell-out, the private sector would be the largest in terms of number of persons engaged and gross output. Under my government, the private sector was the smallest, and there were plans to reduce it even further. The establishment of joint private/government business enterprises, the "N.L.C." stated, would be "purely on a voluntary basis." As for the remaining sectors, active state participation would be limited to "certain basic and key projects", though no details were given; and the activities of the Co-operative movement would be "purely economic". It would "not be allowed to get itself involved in politics". As if to reassure their neo-colonialist masters even more the "N.L.C." went on to say that it had no plans for nationalisation, and would work towards the eventual abolition of import controls from the economy. There was to be a two-year "review period" starting on 1st July 1966, during which there would be "proper economic stocktaking". Even "N.L.C." supporters must have marvelled at the time to be spent on "stocktaking" when the nation was supposed to be in such dire economic trouble. But, according to the "N.L.C.," this was necessary if Ghana was to be in a position to expect "help" from the "outside world".

And the "N.L.C." called this miserable "For Sale" notice an "economic" plan. This was to be their substitute for the Seven Year Development Plan with its positive constructive detailed proposals for the economic emancipation of Ghana.

However, it brought results in the shape of the usual hand-outs granted by imperialists and neo-colonialists to well-behaved puppets. Within two weeks of the ending of legal government in Ghana, the army and police traitors received an invitation to send a mission to Washington for talks with the International Monetary Fund and World Bank officials. The upshot was a £13 million stand-by credit received from the I.M.F. and eventually new loans from the U.S.A., Canada and West Germany. In addition, supplies of various foodstuffs and other consumer goods were promised to provide the necessary window dressing for the new regime.

In the recent wave of coups which have taken place in Asia, Latin America and Africa, all this has come to be standard practice. Wherever progressive governments have been re-placed by counter-revolutionary forces, imperialist financial organisations have rushed to bolster them up with loans and various forms of so-called "aid". It is a necessary corollary to the "big lie" usually employed to justify the overthrow of "undesirable governments"—the lie of "economic chaos" and a "starving" population. But more important, it serves to tighten the stranglehold of foreign economic control over the captive people by creating more indebtedness and a deeper penetration by foreign business interests.

The Economic Committee set up by the "N.L.C." admitted in a statement on 3rd March 1966 that Ghana's economy was "basically strong", and that a mere £15 million was all that was needed to overcome immediate difficulties. Yet members of the Economic Committee went like beggars, cap in hand, for talks in Washington, London, Bonn and other capitals greedily snatching any niggardly hand-outs offered, and cravenly agree-ing to all kinds of conditions attached to them. During talks in London in June1966, it was announced that nine public cor-porations were to be handed over to private enterprise; and investors, both local and foreign, were to be invited to join in the running of six others.

On that occasion, the Committee was discussing Ghana's economy with 13 Western creditor countries, and asking for their agreement on the re-scheduling of capital and interest payments. The Committee only managed to get their agree-ment to report back to their governments and the promise of a further meeting "in due course". I wonder if the Committee paused to reflect then on the different attitude of our creditors among the socialist countries. These had granted Ghana an unconditional moratorium on capital and interest payments, knowing that the slump in the price of cocoa had been the main cause of our borrowing, and that our difficulties were only temporary. My government had made certain economies, but had rejected Western demands for drastic cuts in publicly-owned industries which we regarded as vital to economic independence.

Apart from handing over public corporations to private enterprise, the "N.L.C." announced drastic cuts in the routes operated by Ghana Airways, the halting of work on the new international airport at Tamale in Northern Ghana, and the cancellation of a number of orders for new ships for the state-owned Black Star Line. Both Ghana Airways and the Black Star Line were established by my government to break the monopoly of foreign transport companies. They were ultimately to become foreign currency earners.

At Afienya, some 26 miles from Accra, the "N.L.C." shut down the excellent Gliding School established by Flight Captain Hanna Reitsch. The School, recognised as among the best in the world, was providing valuable initial flying training for members of the Young Pioneers, Army and Air Force cadets, and for trainees from other African countries.

The excuse was made that these were all prestige projects. The same excuse was given as the reason for abandoning or selling to private ownership other important state enterprises, though everyone knows that they were surrendered because they threatened the business interests of the new masters of Ghana—the neo-colonialists and their agents. The foundation of new industries and the building up of national air and ship-ping lines is seen as evidence of prestige spending only by imperialists and neo-colonialists who wish to see a country revert back to the position of a colony.

The Juapong Textile and Knitting factory near Akosombo in the Volta Region, was one of the many vital development projects to be abandoned during the first few months of "N.L.C." rule. This factory, half completed when the army and police traitors seized power, was to offer employment to over 800 people, and to make use of 400,000 tons of locally-produced cotton from the Abutia, Chinderi and Zongo Mancheri state farms. The factory, when completed, was expected to produce over 80,000 tons of textiles of various kinds annually, and about 3,000 tons of knitwear. It was the only industry sited by the government in the Volta Region, and suspension of work on it therefore caused bitter disappointment locally, and resulted in a great waste of time, energy and money. A writer in the *Ghanaian Times* visited the site towards the end of 1966 and reported "the whole area desolate, with the half-completed buildings almost overgrown with weeds". The project had been started by Chinese experts, and when these were sent home no attempt was made to continue with the work.

Another example of the stupidity of sending away much-needed specialists from socialist countries may be seen in the "N.L.C.'s" decision to return the 29 Russian-built fishing trawlers which had been lying idle since the departure of the Soviet technicians. And this when the people of Ghana badly need an increase in the protein content of their diet. Later, as a result of protests, the "N.L.C." declared their intention to sell the trawlers to private interests.

Some 2,500 Russian and Chinese experts were expelled from Ghana by the "N.L.C.," regardless of the invaluable services they were rendering to the economic development of the country. The "N.L.C." had stated that it was "non-aligned" yet it callously sacrificed the interests of the people by abandoning precious economic projects simply for political reasons. Even the imperialist press was moved to remark: "The new regime is pledged to pursue a policy of non-alignment while being friendly with all. But there is no mistaking the fair breeze blowing towards the Western camp at the moment" (*Daily Telegraph,* 10th March 1966).

All projects or schemes developed by Soviet or Chinese experts, and also several undertaken by specialists from other socialist countries, were suspended, abandoned entirely, or sold to foreign capitalists. Small wonder William H. Beaty, Vice-President of the Chase Manhattan Bank of the U.S.A., was quick to visit Ghana and spoke of the "favourable investment conditions" owing to the "remarkable strides" which had been made since 24th February 1966. Like his counterparts in other capitalist countries, he doubtless regarded Ghana under the "N.L.C." as just another client state set up to sustain

101

imperialism, neo-colonialism and the capitalist economies of the West.

Traitors among our own people are helping in the sell-out. Seeing the opportunity to make quick money, some of them have become "market analysts" for prospective investors. Perhaps they hope the grand-sounding name may disguise the fact that they are raking in vast sums of money by acting as middle-men in the disgraceful and indiscriminate disposal of Ghana's state property to private enterprise. Their task has been made easy by the encouragement of prospective investors by advertisements of the Capital Investments Board. They have been promised generous concessions, including a ten-year tax holiday and the free transfer abroad of profits after the payment of any tax due. What a paradise for neo-colonial-ists—the free transfer abroad of profits and a tax holiday; and all this without any strings attached. In their wildest dreams they could not have hoped for better conditions, even from the servile "N.L.C."

Under my government, there was strict control of the operations of all foreign firms in Ghana. We were constantly vigilant to see that there was no exploitation of the Ghanaian people, and that most of the profits were retained inside Ghana to be used to promote further economic and social development.

In Ghana today it is as though the clock suddenly stopped on 24th February 1966, and the hands have been turned backwards. Unfinished factory buildings remain in precisely the same condition as when the builders left them after work on 23rd February 1966. The machines of other factories, said to be prestige projects or closed because of the departure of foreign technicians, lie idle while thousands of Ghanaian unemployed fill the streets. Work on new schools, hospitals, roads and airport buildings has stopped, the new regime making the excuse that the country is too poor to pay for them. The cars and property of Party officials have been sold; where the money has gone, only the "N.L.C." can tell.

My personal Research Office, where documents of all kinds were being filed, and valuable records were being built up, was ransacked, and the painstaking work of many years destroyed. Many thousands of books in my library were sense-lessly torn up or burnt.

102

Housing schemes have been abandoned. For example, work has been stopped on the manufacture of prefabricated houses which were being built to relieve the acute housing shortage. Some of the vital services have been neglected, such as water purification and insecticide spraying, both essential for the health of the people and for the keeping down of insect pests. Locusts have once again become a problem. They had not been seen in Ghana since 1933. Health facilities of all kinds have been allowed to run down, and many doctors have resigned. The "N.L.C." even deported from Ghana the distinguished United States medical expert Dr. Anna Livia Cordero who had come from Puerto Rico to help with our public health services. Though she held the highest medical diplomas the rebel regime would not allow her to continue work in Ghana because of her criticisms of their policy.

State farms, rubber and cotton plantations, and other rural development projects have been allowed to fall into decay, and valuable crops lost due to lack of attention. Large quantities of cocoa are being smuggled out of Ghana, with disastrous effects on the economy.

The only Ghanaians to benefit from the sell-out and the surrender to imperialism have been the bourgeois elements and a small number of hoarders and profiteers determined to cash-in on the free-for-all. For the ordinary men and women of Ghana it has meant a return to all the exploitation and uncertainties of colonial days.

They were faced almost at once with widespread unemployment. Since 24th February 1966, many thousands have been thrown out of work. The figure given in the pro-"N.L.C." magazine *West Africa* (22nd April 1967) was 105,000. In relation to population and potential labour force, Ghana now has the highest unemployment rate of any country in the world. There is 30 per cent. unemployment in Accra alone. Never before has Ghana experienced anything like the mass unemployment resulting from "N.L.C." misrule and mismanagement. Apart from the men and women thrown out of work from state factories and farms, thousands more have been dismissed from the Workers Brigade and other organisations. To these have been added Party officials, T.U.C. employees, newspaper reporters and editors, employees of the Bureau of African Affairs, the African Affairs Centre and similar organisations. Hundreds have been expelled from schools and colleges because they supported socialism and the programme of African liberation and unity.

Coupled with the distress caused by mass unemployment and the victimisation of supporters of the legal government, came sharp rises in the prices of certain essential foods. Prices are still rising and the standard of living is falling drastically. Some commodities have disappeared entirely from shops and markets as profiteers hoard supplies. There is a flourishing black market. Many of the police have become personally involved in the racketeering, forcing traders to sell them goods at a low price and then re-selling them at exorbitant rates. Bribery and corruption, as foreign visitors have been quick to report, have begun to penetrate every corner.

In May 1967, Kofi Akyigyina, an Accra businessman, revealed to the Jiagge Commission that certain top-ranking police officers were engaged in private business. He told how four senior police officers had teamed up with a few other persons to operate a multi-lateral company in Ghana for the manufacture of milk powder, shirts, soda and furniture. The company was also to deal in industrial and commercial diamonds, diamond products, and to construct roads and bridges. Financiers from the U.S.A. were expected to assist. Akyigyina said that directors of the company actually held their meetings at Police Headquarters in Accra, and that in April 1967 two Italian businessmen were interviewed by the directors of the company, again at Police Headquarters.

As a result of these disclosures, and to prevent any further adverse publicity, Deputy Commissioners of Police, E. K. Levi and A. K. Biney, and Chief Superintendents G. C. Tay and G. K. Acheampong were dismissed from the Police Service.

The "N.L.C.," pressing ahead with what it called "austerity" measures repeatedly urged Ghanaians to tighten their belts and to make sacrifices. But they were being asked to suffer for no apparent reason. There had been times of stringency under my government, but then they knew the reasons for it. All around they could see evidence of building and development. They knew they were helping to implement the Seven Year Development Plan which would ultimately bring economic independence and a big rise in their standard of living. After 24th February 1966, however, they saw the abandonment of development projects, the departure of foreign experts on which many of the new industries depended, and the wholesale selling of state-owned enterprises to private investors. They noted the sudden influx of British, American, Israeli and West German businessmen; and the way that the U.S. and British ambassadors practically live at the Castle, where the "N.L.C." has its administrative headquarters. They moved to the Castle from Police Headquarters for greater safety.

Instead of the accent being on development there seemed to be nothing but destruction and negative policies—a pulling down process. The ordinary people of Ghana were told to tighten their belts and to make sacrifices so that foreign businessmen and their local stooges could grow fat on the exploitation of Ghana's resources and on the proceeds of Ghanaian labour.

The puppet press and radio reflecting the official line poured out a steady stream of abuse against me personally and against my government. Endless commissions of enquiry were set up, manned by members of the old opposition and various other ambitious men anxious to ingratiate themselves with the new regime. Staged public hearings were given to previously-prepared witnesses, to which correspondents of the foreign and local press were invited. The testimony of these so-called witnesses was claimed to be incontrovertible proof of the "wickedness" of my government. As fast as one commission ended its work another was set up. It seemed the "N.L.C." was desperate to keep up a constant flow of invective, and often filthy abuse, for the subservient press and radio to publicise. The majority of Ghanaians became sickened by the whole process. Most of the mud stuck to the hands of the throwers.

A particularly nauseating part of the smear campaign was the putting of a dead woman and child into the refrigerator at Flagstaff House, saying that this was "Kwame Nkrumah's juju", and inviting public inspection. The woman and child were among those murdered on 24th February. But the public turned the open invitation to Flagstaff House into a kind of pilgrimage and the inspection offer had to be quickly withdrawn.

The attacks on me personally began as soon as it was known that I had gone to Guinea and intended returning to Ghana to restore legal government. Having declared on 24th February 1966 that "the myth of Kwame Nkrumah has been destroyed" they showed that they thought it still very much alive, by launching an all-out attack on me in the press and on the radio. I am, it seems, a Hitler, a Lenin, a Bluebeard, a Mao Tse-tung, a Tsar, a Leninist Tsar, a miser, a spendthrift, and latterly, a criminal, guilty of "murder and conspiracy", with a price of £50,000 on my head.

Western newspapers and periodicals, particularly in the U.S., Britain and West Germany, also maintain a barrage of abuse. In attacks of unprecedented ferocity, I am accused of practically every character fault imaginable. The falseness of the accusations, and the personal nature of the charges, make me wonder if the writers and editors have adopted this method of attack because they are unable to challenge or refute my political ideas and philosophy or the consistency of my efforts for the attainment of African continental freedom and an All-African Union Government.

In the notices of "wanted men" put up outside police stations in Ghana in January 1967, full details were given of my physical appearance and career as though I were a common criminal, and as if Ghanaians had never heard of me. The authors of the notice made themselves look even more ridiculous by saying that I had been imprisoned "for political offences" in 1950! If I hadn't seen the notices myself I would have found it hard to believe they could have made such a laughing-stock of themselves.

I had, according to the "N.L.C." and their stooges, quite a record. But not, I think, the record by which I am judged by the people of Ghana and of Africa. They know me. They know the kind of life I lead, and the goals for which I strive. I make no defence. I make no apology. I do not consider myself on trial. But for the benefit of foreign critics who may have swallowed probably the most vicious lie of all—that I have built up a large personal fortune, I must add that the "N.L.C." has itself had to admit that the allegation is false and untrue.

As each day has passed, unemployment, strikes, rioting and crime of all kinds have increased in Ghana. The local press

106

began to report some of the most sensational facts and figures. But steps were soon taken by the "N.L.C." to suppress the publication of any adverse news and comment. Early in October 1966 it issued what have come to be called the "Rumours Decrees" to muzzle the press and to give the police the power to arrest and detain without warrant. Decree 92 made it an offence, punishable with up to three years imprisonment, to publish anything "likely to cause alarm and despondency . . . . disturb the public peace . . . . or cause disaffection against the N.L.C." My own government had enacted legislation to deal with rumour mongering. In a country where many people were still unfortunately illiterate, dangerous rumours can be circulated and obtain wide currency. For example, there was a rumour that because on a new bank note issued no date appeared, the notes in question were valueless and we used this legislation to deal with those who put round such stories when we knew them to be false. The "N.L.C." decrees are of quite a different sort. They were aimed at the press and at their supporters who were beginning to see through the pretensions of the military and timidly to expose them.

Editors and journalists who were employed under my government were dismissed, and most of them imprisoned soon after the army and police traitors seized power. Party editors were seized, beaten up and flung into prison. But their replacements are not proving easy to control. After the arrest of the Editors-in-Chief of the *Evening News* and the *Ghanaian Times,* two formerly-detained journalists were appointed to replace them—Henry Thompson and K. Y. Attoh. They began by dismissing journalists said to be orientated towards socialism and Nkrumaism, and their authority was bolstered up by daily visits of armed soldiers to the Guinea Press. But before long, Thompson and Attoh began to criticise the new regime. Thompson campaigned for an early return to civil government, and called for a halt to the raiding, looting and burning of Workers Brigade Camps. Attoh, for his part, protested against the destoolment of 194 chiefs and their replacement by "N.L.C." puppets. Jointly, they attacked profiteering and other malpractices, and exposed the tribalism and backward-sliding of the "N.L.C." The result has been the appointment of a new Chief Editor for the whole Press, Moses Danquah, though it is doubtful if he will prove any more co-operative.

Bob Bannerman, who worked at the Guinea Press for 8 years, and continued working there for a further three months after the army-police insurrection, has written from the safety of London about how the "N.L.C." took over the Press in Ghana:

> "Despite the appeal of the 'N.L.C.' clique, few people turned out for work on the first day. When it was later learnt that the army bandits planned to set fire to the Press, we had no alternative but to surrender, and publish the numerous decrees of the illegal clique, including anti-Nkrumah letters manufactured by the 'N.L.C.' and purporting to come from readers."

Bannerman describes the arrival of army units at the Press, the dismissals and threats, and the resulting apparent subservience. He continues:

> "The dismissal of professional journalists like G. T. Anim, General Manager of the Ghana News Agency, and E. Coleman, Director of Broadcasting, came later, but the replacements of the 'N.L.C.' were so bad that they threaten the entire Press, T.V., and Radio network in Ghana. In fact the entire profession has been paralysed."

The Chairman of the Ghana Broadcasting Service, Cecil Forde, has been arrested and detained. Many journalists and workers of the External Broadcasting Department have been dismissed because they supported programmes on African unity, and because they were not Ghanaians, though they were Africans. This was in line with orders from the U.S. Embassy in Accra, to root out all possible sources of criticism of U.S. imperialism, and to chase all progressive non-Ghanaian Africans from Ghana.

Foreign correspondents of TASS, Izvestia and Pravda were attacked openly and their offices closed down. The correspondent of the New China News Agency (Hsinhua) also received rough treatment. He had published descriptions of the assaults made on foreign journalists and technicians.

However, propaganda teams from Britain and the United States have full access to all Press establishments, and the U.S. Press attaché visits the Guinea Press at least twice a day.

The few foreign journalists from socialist countries who have managed to continue to operate in Ghana are gradually being forced to leave as they find it impossible to refrain from writing the truth about the "N.L.C." In November 1966, Karl-Heinz Grafe, Accra correspondent of A.D.N., the East German News Agency, was deported from Ghana for adverse comment on the military-police dictatorship—and yet the "N.L.C." claims to have abolished censorship. So-called Press freedom clearly only extends to those willing to conceal the truth, and to write nothing but praise.

An amusing example of "press freedom" as it exists under the "N.L.C." was Ankrah's address to the journalists. He was annoyed when the Arab-Israeli war broke out that the Ghana press should have reported it so extensively. He pointed out to them that it was none of their duty and went on to say that after all the government paid them and that "he who pays the piper must call the tune".

Probably one of the most criminal and stupid acts of the "N.L.C" to date has been the setting up of military tribunals "to try expeditiously certain categories of subversive offences committed by non-military personnel, conviction for any of which will carry a maximum sentence of death by a firing squad and a minimum of not less than 25 years with hard labour".

This decree, known as the Armed Forces Act (1962) Amended Decree (1967) states that any person who prepared or endeavoured to produce by force any alteration of the law or the policies of the "N.L.C.," or incited, or without lawful authority had in possession, custody or control any explosives, firearms or ammunition, should be guilty of the offence of subversion. The decree also declared that any person who organised or incited any other person to go on a general strike likely to cause the overthrow of the "N.L.C." would equally be guilty of subversion. Other activities covered by the decree included the publishing of any statement or report which the person knew to be false, and which was likely to undermine the confidence of the people of Ghana in the permanency of "their newly-won freedom". The decree covered the killing or the attempt to kill, or the conspiring with any other person to kill any member of the "N.L.C.," or any Ghanaian citizen with a view to overthrowing the "N.L.C." Any person with

knowledge of any of the foregoing acts who did not report it
to the authorities immediately, was also to be considered guilty
of subversion. A military tribunal should consist of the pre-
siding officer, who should be an officer of the Armed Forces
not below the rank of Brigadier in the Ghana Army, or its
equivalent in the Ghana Navy or Air Force. It should also
consist of four other members, all of whom should be officers
of the Ghana Armed Forces not below the rank of Major in
the Ghana Army or its equivalent in the other two services.
The decree finally stipulated that the decision of the military
tribunal should be final, and that no appeal should arise from
such a decision.

This amendment of the Armed Forces Act was published
by the "N.L.C." on 30th January 1967. It reveals the depths
to which the "N.L.C." had sunk and showed that they had
almost reached the end of their tether. By imposing what virtually amounted to martial law it admitted for all to see that it
could no longer keep in check the growing opposition to rule
by the army and police clique. In giving reasons for the establishment of military tribunals, the "N.L.C" mentioned activities by a "small minority" of former Party members. The
severity of the measures taken against them hardly squares
with the assertion of insignificant numbers, but then the
"N.L.C." has not been noted for consistency or good sense.

The "N.L.C.," on assuming power, encountered immediate
lack of co-operation from the judiciary. After a few months
they dismissed all judges and magistrates appointed under
ny government, and installed others whom they thought they
could count on to give favourable verdicts. It has become
clear, by the resort to martial law, that even the tame judiciary
cannot be relied on to act sufficiently swiftly and decisively to
quell the mounting opposition.

The quality of the tame judiciary may be judged from the
muddled thinking displayed by Edward Akuffo-Addo,
appointed Chief Justice of Ghana by the "N.L.C.", when he
stated: "We do not subscribe to the sovereignty of Parliament. We subscribe to the sovereignty of law." What in fact
he was saying was that sovereign power rested with the judiciary, and not with the law-making body. Making himself
appear even more ridiculous, he went on to state that he saw
"no biological sanction" for giving the vote at 21, and that

110

he envisaged some kind of quality vote based on "literacy" and "intelligence"—in other words, an abandonment of the cardinal principle of true democracy: one man, one vote.

Thousands of Ghanaians still remain, without trial, in prisons and detention camps. Countless others go in daily fear of arrest. But the imperialist press is silent on these matters. It has not reported the wholesale dismissal of judges and magistrates, the establishment of military tribunals, nor the strikes, boycotts, riots and other evidence of suffering and unrest. Its readers have not been told of the abolition of the free medical service, nor of the cuts in spending on education. We do not expect otherwise—it is almost war.

Of course, like the leaders of all counter-revolutionary military coups, the "N.L.C." proclaimed that its intention was to hand over to civilians as soon as satisfactory arrangements could be made. And in common with their counterparts in other countries, the military and police traitors are never likely to do this. Having seized power by force they find themselves in an entirely false position. Knowing they do not represent the mass of the people, they dare not hold elections or referendums. Yet to survive they must keep up the charade of wanting a return to civilian rule by setting up constitutional commissions to prepare the way.

For months, the Constitutional Commission set up by the "N.L.C." held meetings, but no progress was reported. Ghanaians were invited to send suggestions for a new constitution to the Commission. The response was negligible, and the people were accused by the "N.L.C." of "apathy". On 12th January 1967, it was announced that the Constitutional Commission would divide into three working groups and would undertake an extensive tour of the Regions "to receive memoranda and oral representations from all sections of the community". There is no evidence to suggest that this venture was any more successful.

With its back to the wall, the Liar's Council announced on 22nd May 1968 that it hoped there would be a return to civilian rule by 30th September 1969. It was announced that elections for the Constituent Assembly, the body to be responsible for finalising the new constitution for Ghana, would be on a non-party basis. In other words, there was to be no lifting of the ban on political activity until after the Constituent

Assembly had completed its work and the new constitution had been promulgated and imposed on the people of Ghana.

In denying the right of Ghanaians to hold popular elections for the establishing of the Constituent Assembly, the "N.L.C." showed that it was not even prepared to carry out the recommendations of its own Constitutional Commission. The latter recommended that the Constituent Assembly should be established "by popular elections", and that "it should be the people's representative body in a truly democratic sense".

According to the published draft constitutional proposals there was to be an all-powerful Judiciary. The "President" was to have under his "control" and "supervision" certain organs and departments of government which were to be virtually independent of the government of the day. He was to be assisted by an appointed, not elected, Council of State. An Elections and Public Offices Disqualification Decree banned thousands of Ghanaians from holding public office for ten years because they were members of the C.P.P. and believed in socialism.

Those who overthrew the constitutional government of Ghana on 24th February 1966 cannot avoid the consequences of their treachery, or the inescapable fact that the vast majority of Ghanaians are against them. They can neither remain in power indefinitely, nor organise a return to civilian rule.

It is unrealistic to imagine that a neo-colonialist military regime which seized power by force will hand over to a "civilian government" through a "general election". They may talk of "free elections" and "an early return to civilian rule", but this is simply to deceive the masses and to discourage resistance. The only effective solution lies in revolutionary action in the form of a counter-coup, that is to say, a decisive reversal of the original coup.

7

AWAKENING

The unremitting, though ineffectual, attacks made by the military and police traitors on my government and on myself may be partly explained by the strength of the resistance they encountered. Right from the start, men and women began to meet secretly to talk about what had taken place and to discuss what should be done. Loyal members of the Party began to organise underground resistance. Soon posters and slogans began to appear on walls of buildings in Accra and elsewhere, calling on the people to rise up and overthrow the traitors. Leaflets were printed and distributed, though restrictions were placed on the sale of paper, and the police instructed sellers to take the names and addresses of anyone purchasing an unusual amount of stationery. Ghanaians had a rude awakening as they began to experience the bitter consequences of the overthrow of the constitutional government and "N.L.C." treachery.

In London, two organisations went into immediate action: the Overseas Branch of the Party, and the Socialist Ghana Defence Committee. They began a campaign to inform the public of the true state of affairs in Ghana. I quote the statement issued by the Party Overseas:

> An illegal military rebellion has taken place in Ghana and is trying to seize power.
> The Convention People's Party Overseas regard this not only as a rebellion of leading military figures and reactionaries inside the country who have long opposed the progressive steps taken by President Nkrumah and his Government, but that it is also supported and even organised by the most reactionary forces outside Ghana.
> The rebellion in Ghana is occurring after similar

113

incidents have taken place in other parts of Africa. It can therefore be seen as part of the same onslaught which has been sweeping the African continent. This offensive is directed against progressive African leaders who have been successfully resisting attempts by the imperialist powers to exploit their countries.

We consider the aim of the present campaign in Ghana is to set up a typical neo-colonialist regime which will be subsidiary to foreign imperialism. It will renounce, in fact, whatever it may pretend on the surface, the independence won with such sacrifice by thousands of Ghanaians with great men like Kwame Nkumah in the leadership.

The Convention People's Party's Overseas do not recognise this so-called regime. The rebellion is regrettably being made out as a liberal democratic movement. It is not. It is an extreme right-wing movement which, if allowed to entrench itself, will turn the clock of progress many years back in Ghana.

Osagyefo Dr. Kwame Nkrumah remains the legal President and the constitutional head of the Republic of Ghana. His legal government remains and will take up its authority again. We therefore call upon the British Government, and all governments for that matter, not to recognise the so-called National Liberation Council.

In the meantime, the Party Overseas remains organised and at its post and calls for the continued support of all loyal Ghanaians for the legally elected leader, Osagyefo Dr. Kwame Nkrumah.

Ekow Eshun,
Secretary of the Party, Overseas.
(Issued in London on 24th February 1966).

In January 1967, another organisation, the People's Progressive Front of Ghana, was formed in London to oppose the "N.L.C." and particularly their collaborators from among the reactionary, old "opposition" elements.

Reports reach me daily of mounting disorder and discontent in Ghana. Some of this is due to straightforward economic hardship caused by the abandonment of the Seven Year

Development Plan, mass unemployment and rising prices, but most of it has a strong political undercurrent. This was admitted by the "N.L.C." in a broadcast to the workers in December 1966. They spoke of what they called "unreasonable strikes" and the "subversive elements" behind them. Among the innumerable strikes was one at W. Biney and Company at Tema, where some 2,000 workers were involved and armed troops had to intervene. Soon, it was found necessary to gaol strike leaders. In August 1966, more than 400 workers at the Ghana Textile Manufacturing Company went on strike and three of the leaders were sentenced to 12 months' imprisonment on charges of inciting the workers. The Ghana Trades Union Congress, then under "N.L.C." stooge control, warned workers throughout the country against what it called " a growing tendency" to strike. It is not possible to include mention here of every strike that has occurred, but hardly a week has gone by without a report of some major strike. Early in December 1966, 5,000 miners of Ashanti Goldfields Corporation in Obuasi downed tools for four days and only returned to work when their full demands had been met. Naturally, the strikers always give non-political reasons for their action, but their behaviour is clearly seen by the "N.L.C." as evidence of a nation-wide campaign of civil disobedience and sabotage.

Strikes have not been confined to factories, mines and farms. Schoolchildren and students are joining in the protest against the actions of the "N.L.C." It was made plain as soon as the traitors seized power, that education was to be one of the first of the public services to be cut. Free schooling was abolished, and parents were told that they would have in future to pay for all school text-books. Building was stopped on several new schools, including two big new secondary schools in the Volta Region, and many state schools were sold to private ownership. The outcry raised by the handing over of several schools, in some cases to unqualified people, caused the "N.L.C." to stop the process, but not before much confusion had been caused. Even the docile press reported cases of schoolchildren "striking," "rioting" and indulging in "disorderly behaviour". The editorial in the *Ghanaian Times* of 15th June 1966, headed "Secondary School Riotings" began: "We are dismayed by the reports of yet another outbreak of rioting and vandalism by secondary school boys and girls . . . . First

115

it was a school at Koforidua, next it was in Accra, and now from the noise and bustle of Accra and Koforidua the trouble has moved to the quiet hill-town of Aburi, where the boys and girls of the Adonten Secondary School rioted at midnight last Sunday." According to the report, they caused damage to school property estimated at 2,400 cedis. No explanation is given of the sudden urge of our children "to maim and destroy" as the editor of the *Ghanaian Times* put it, though right at the end of the editorial there is a hint that the trouble might be political since "some teachers" had been trained at the Ideological Institute in Winneba.

In January 1967, I received news of the closing of the Akropong Teacher Training College due to "lack of teachers and pupils". If this was the case, it could be for only one reason —the determination of all concerned to join in the campaign of strikes and boycotts aimed at overthrowing the "N.L.C." On 12th November 1966, about 300 students at Cape Coast University College staged a demonstration. They carried placards calling for an end to the "N.L.C."

In the daily "Situation Reports" I receive has come news of the stealing of school textbooks at night from the schools. This is not surprising. Textbooks now have to be paid for, and many parents thrown out of work after 24th February 1966 have found themselves also faced with school bills for the first time. Crime of all kinds has increased rapidly. There are even reports of the theft of food, an offence previously unknown in Ghana. In June 1966, conditions in Kumasi were described as "intolerable" because of "hooliganism". Evidently the position did not improve; the deputy superintendent of police in Kumasi, M. P. Agyiri, was dismissed as a scapegoat on 24th January 1967 because it was said that he had neglected his duty and had brought the police service into disrepute.

The "N.L.C." ordered the release of many convicted criminals to make room in the prisons for the thousands of political prisoners, and undoubtedly the activities of some of these men have contributed to the crime wave, but basically the trouble has been caused by genuine hardship, complete contempt for authority in the shape of stooge army and police, and by a determination to bring about the collapse of the "N.L.C."

116

Offences such as "acts tending to disturb the peace" and other similar offences have increased sharply, and the "N.L.C." has shown an equal inability to deal with them. I remember a particularly revealing Situation Report I received on 29th August 1966 concerning a Mr. S. R. Snyper, a locomotive foreman arrested for publicly accusing the "N.L.C." of being a "truly Notorious Liars' Council". Snyper had spoken openly against the "N.L.C." at Sekondi Railway Station. However, after several weeks, it was decided that the case should not be brought before the courts, "to avoid further publicity".

The following short excerpts from Situation Reports illustrate the mounting unrest and hardship in Ghana, and are typical of the kind of information I have received regularly since arriving in Conakry.

18.8.66
   General: In all Regions the trend still remains—a marked increase in cases of burglary during the night. In addition there were:
   1. *Northern Region:* 4 arrests for "Acts tending to disturb peace".
   2. *Brong Ahafo:* 8 arrests for "Acts tending to disturb the peace".

27.8.66
   General: Stealing. Widespread stealing, including the stealing of foodstuffs still prevails in the Regions.

30.8.66
   General: Stealing is widespread in towns and villages all over Ghana. Many cases of "Acts tending to disturb the peace". (Details followed).

1.9.66
   Retrenchment in the Regions: Workers paid off in the Upper Region:
   Zuarangu State Farm Division 306
   Wa State Farm Division 91
   Bolga Young Farmers League 8
None of the laid-off employees have been employed in other fields nor registered in any Labour Centre. Public criticism

of the policy is that unemployment in the country is mounting at an alarming rate.

2.9.66

Item 2. Further laying-off of State farm employees:
According to Assistant Commissioner of Police in the Western Region, 1,281 rubber plantation workers throughout the Region were laid-off on 1st September 1966.

The campaign against so-called "redundant labour" still continues.

Note: This brings the number of State Farm workers affected in the Western Region to 1,380. Thus 684 more workers will be laid-off to reach the original target of 2,064 "retrenched" workers.

6.9.66

General: Widespread cases of stealing in all Regions, including stealing of school textbooks from schools during the night.

7.9.66

Profiteering in Volta Region: One Asare of the Ghana News Agency, based in Peki (Volta Region), has sent a telegram to C.I.D. headquarters in Accra reporting widespread cases of:
(a) selling of essential commodities to general traders.
(b) hoarding.
(c) profiteering.
In his telegram, Asare reported that the Volta Regional Police are aware of these malpractices but are unconcerned.

8.9.66

General: Acts tending to disturb the peace:
(1) Anloga in Volta Region—1 arrest.
(2) Sekondi in Western Region—2 arrests.
Other information of interest:
Location Workers meeting in Sekondi: Western Region Special Branch reports that on 8th September 1966, the Location Branch of Railway Administration and Port Workers Union held an hour's general meeting at Sekondi. Attendance is quoted as being about 1,000. A. Hagan (Branch Vice-Chairman) presided and speakers were G. K. Essien, Kofi and two others.

118

The general themes of the speakers at the meeting were:
(1) Workers were advised not to grumble over the bonuses given to Army and Police after the 24th February rebellion.
(2) Workers were exhorted to stand united and fight for their rights.
(3) Workers were cautioned to refrain from indulgence in politics.

Note: Workers at the meeting are reported to have been disappointed by B. A. Bentum's failure to attend the meeting as originally planned. *The meeting broke up in confusion.*

26.11.66

288 students from the Government Technical Institute, Kikam, used tree trunks to block the road leading to Axim-Essiama main road, and jeered at school instructors. The demonstration was against the newly-appointed Headmaster, whose removal they sought.

10.12.66

Following the suspension of three students from the Presbyterian Training College, Akropong, for "misbehaviour". the other students refused to attend classes. Omanhene of Akropong/Akwapim and elders, appealed to the students to remain calm. Day and night police patrols arranged on the campus . Principal H. T. Dako closing school 10.12.66 instead of 16.12.66 to avoid disturbances.

15.12.66

220 employees of Timber Veneer and Lumber Company, Takoradi (T.V.L.C.), went on strike in protest against the dismissal of T.V.L.C. Workers' Union Chairman. T.U.C. and Labour Office officials intervened, but employees refused to return to work. Management has warned that all workers will be dismissed if strike is not called off. All strikers left for home. (The matter was later referred to the Timber Federation and eventually work was resumed.)

29.11.66

Diamond Mining Corporation at Takorawase closed on 28.11.66. Entire workshop and operation will be stopped. Supervisors will be suspended on 31.12.66 and all employees affected will be laid-off. Situation is serious. Arrangements are being made to safeguard mines properties.

21.12.66

Police warning to all Regions. Information received armed robbers to attack banks in Ghana any time from now. Armed guards must be posted all banks all times.

22.12.66

Inspector General of Police to all Regions. Reliably informed, plot by "nation wreckers" to sabotage electrical installations in country. Immediately place armed guards on all electricity stations in your area, and ensure all other valuable electricity points are well protected.

7.1.67

Takoradi—20 arrested for strike.

13.1.67

Accra to all Borders. Following military coup in Togo, alert all personnel and ensure that strong security measures are taken at all border guard posts and stations to prevent pro-Nkrumah travellers entering Ghana.

14.1.67

250 workers of Prestea, Bondaye and Tuapem branches of State Gold Mining Corporation went on strike today demanding a pay rise of 6 pesewas a day. General Secretary of the Mine Workers' Union (I. N. Aikins) has left Tarkwa for Prestea to handle deteriorating situation.

General Secretary met workers for four hours on 14th January. Workers agreed to call off strike on 16th January on condition Managing Director of Corporation met them. Meanwhile, Police Western Region answering a query from Accra as to action being taken against strikers have intimated that "investigations" are under way which might lead to the prosecution of strike instigators.

16.1.67

Fire broke out at Tamale airfield extension site on 14th January. Considerable damage done buildings and other property. Cause of fire unknown. 15 watchmen have been arrested for interrogation.

General Information:

1. Ex-Security Officers continue to be arrested in Ghana:
   (a) John Apeadu arrested Axim, 16th January.
   (b) Walter Sugget Cudjoe arrested Bibiani, 17th January.
   (c) George Kwesi Essien arrested Western Region, 19th January.

2. Sampson Sasu Baffour-Awuah, a 26-year-old storekeeper, is wanted for treason. The hunt for him is now on a national scale. Subject "is wanted urgently by police who believe he has valuable information in connection with an important investigation".

3. Robbery in Ghana has now assumed gangster proportions, and often involves armed robbers in police and army uniforms. On 9th January, a large amount of store goods stolen from Makola.

4. Recently, over 800 policemen of all ranks in all regions have been drastically reshuffled by widespread transfers at short notice. Some policemen openly defied threats of dismissal and opposed their short notice transfers. The move was obviously meant to curb "uniformed" robbery by moving policemen from their regions.

21.1.67

Two cases of robbery at Kyekyewere and Jacobu villages at dawn by unknown thieves, two dressed in army uniforms. Properties involved cash 2,304.00 cedis and personal effects, value 432.00 cedis. No recovery. No arrest.

24.1.67

Aburi: Kingsley Asiam, former M.P. and member of the proscribed C.P.P., arrested at Nsawam by soldiers under command of Capt. W. T. Addy, in connection with abortive counter-revolutionary coup. Brought to Aburi station en route to Accra. Subject was said to have warned Rev. Ekuban on 8.1.67 against attacking disbanded C.P.P. during a ceremony at funeral service of late Madam Dina Donkor, a former staunch member of disbanded C.P.P. He was arrested on orders of Major Osei Owusu.

24.1.67

Wenchi (Brong Ahafo):

(1) Poisoning of water with D.D.T. Two arrests.

(2) Damage by fire to number of houses at Tanoso village. Cause of fire unknown. No arrest.

28.1.67

From Special Branch Headquarters to Western Region: Collect passports of D. K. Foevi and wife, as well as wives of five persons taken into custody, and forward them to Special Branch headquarters.

(The "N.L.C." was withdrawing passports of all persons released from protective custody.)

28.1.67

Ashanti: Robbery at Bomso village on 26th January involving cash, 1,320.00 cedis, and D.-B. gun, value 96.00 cedis. Six men in Mercedes Benz Car NG 1401, colour ash, alleged dressed in police inspector's uniform and army uniforms, conducted search on the premises of Yaw Baasare and made off with loot. No recovery.

2.2.67

Northern Region: Capt. Acquah of 5th Battalion enlisted assistance of Tamale Police effect arrest of ex-Northern Secretary General of disbanded C.P.P. and three ex-D.C.'s of old regime for allegedly holding secret meetings. Accused persons taken to 5th Battalion headquarters for interrogation.

6.2.67

Evidence of Army and Police friction: Mr. K. Avorkliyah of Dormaa Ahenkro reports that he was arrested on 24th January at Nkrankwanta road by Lt. Gyasi and 7 others when he was returning from duty at Nkrankwanta, and his money (238.00 cedis) seized. Next day he was escorted by an army sergeant and a private to Army Camp, Sunyani, where he was detained. He was interrogated and later permitted to return to his station.

11.2.67

It is directed that travel documents of Mr. Chinebuah, Principal Secretary to Ministry of Labour, be impounded. Chinebuah should be refused exit if he attempts to leave Ghana, and Director, Special Branch informed.

12.2.67

Ashanti: Two police mobile patrolmen stopped a vehicle at New Tafo for motor offence. An army officer, one Akinka, arrived at scene and intervened on behalf of driver. Misunderstanding arose between officer and policeman. Army officer became annoyed and pulled out a pistol with a view to shooting constable. More policemen and civilians rushed to scene. Army officer entered his car and drove away. No arrest.

28.2.67

10th Ghana Independence Day to be marked merely by Church Services on 5th March, and Muslim prayers on 3rd March.

28.2.67

All persons released from protective custody are to report to the police from time to time. An "N.L.C." decree published today states such persons are to report themselves direct to police officer in charge of police station nearest to place they usually reside. A released person might alternatively be required to report at such a place as Inspector General of Police might direct. Any released person contravening provisions of the Decree would be guilty of an offence, and would on conviction be liable to a fine not exceeding 400 cedis or a term of imprisonment not exceeding one year, or both.

7.3.67

To Police all Regions: N.L.C. Decree 144. Open separate register at each police post, station or district. First 2 pages of register to contain full list of persons released from protective custody in such particular area. Then rule register showing name, residential address, date and time of person reporting. Also provide column for signature or thumbprint of person concerned, and signature of officer to whom reported. Report should be made once a week. Monthly return of such reports should be forwarded to C.I.D. not later than 10th of ensuing month.

7.3.67

Shooting incident in Accra on 6.3.67, in which one Nigerian was killed. Private Kwakumey of Ghana Army arrested and placed under police custody. 15 other soldiers also involved and placed under military custody. 52 Nigerians concerned with incident being interrogated.

7.3.67

Report from Police/Wiawso: Plot on hand to assassinate Inspector Okpattah in Bibiani District. Demanding immediate protective measures, and early transfer from the District.

8.3.67

At 08.20 hrs. on 6.3.67, No. 6957 To/3 J.Y. Gyamfi of R. H. Koforidua arrested and brought to Koforidua charge office, one Kwame Ansah, a farmer, who was found wearing a white round neck singlet with effigy of deposed President Kwame Nkrumah and inscription "One continent one people". Suspect was reported to have stated that he is one of the subversionists supporting Kwame Nkrumah. Suspect has since been taken into custody for investigations.

20.3.67

From Special Branch/Upper Region to Special Branch/ Headquarters. Students of Pusiga Training College reported demonstrated evening of 17.3.67 at College compound. Number of students involved and cause of demonstration not yet ascertained. No damage to property nor injury to life. Situation presently quiet. Full report will follow.

20.3.67

From Iddrisu Seni Tamale to Prographic/Accra Water shortage. Most severe water shortage which Tamale, the capital of Northern Region has experienced for at least the past four years has hit Tamale and its surrounding villages this year. For the past five days, water has not been flowing into the pipes in some sections of the town and villages. Women and workers find it difficult to get even a bucket of water for either cooking or for washing down their bodies. Mr. Karimu Wemah, Assistant Chief Engineer of the Water and Sewerage Corporation in charge of Northern Region, told the Graphic in an interview that the shortage of water in the Region was due to lack of spare parts to service the machines.

13.4.67

From Police/West Region to Police/Accra Half Assini —Assault on two pump attendants at Half Assini by nine soldiers of 1st Battalion Infantry on operational duties. 5 persons admitted to Axim hospital. No arrest.

RG/Tarkwa—Train derailment at Awaso level crossing involving engine No. 19 MD. 4 persons killed on the spot and 4 seriously injured, admitted B.A.C. Hospital, Awaso. Cause of derailment not yet known.

At 6 a.m. on 17th April, 1967 came the dramatic announcement on Ghana Radio that a three-member military junta had seized power and that the "N.L.C." had been dissolved. For four hours it seemed that Lieutenant Samuel Arthur, the leader of the counter-coup, was firmly in control. He had entered Accra from Ho the previous evening with some 120 men of the Recce Squadron, and had in the early hours of the morning of the 17th captured the radio station, Flagstaff House, and entered Christianborg Castle, the administrative headquarters of the "N.L.C." Then, with equal suddenness a radio announcement declared that the counter-coup had failed, and that Lt. Arthur and his men were under arrest.

At first, the "N.L.C." tried to make light of the attempt to overthrow them. It was said that only a very small section of the army was involved, and that they had received no public support. While admitting that there had been heavy fighting at Christianborg Castle, they gave no casualty figures, and it was not until the evening of the 17th that Kotoka's death was confirmed. There were repeated denials that the attempted counter-coup had anything to do with the C.P.P. or myself. Yet the "N.L.C.", by their own actions, showed that they believed quite the contrary to be the case. In addition to the thousands already in prison, some 489 Party members who had been imprisoned and subsequently released after the original "coup" on 24 February 1966 were re-arrested and imprisoned; and as police reports show, arrests of people said to have taken part in scenes of jubilation early on the morning of the 17th April, were still being carried out several months after the event.

As for the armed forces, the "N.L.C." dared not admit openly how deeply disaffection had penetrated, though here again, as in the case of civilian participation, indirect admission was made by the imprisonment of over 200 soldiers and five senior officers. No officer was promoted to replace

125

Kotoka; Ankrah himself took over the various posts previously held by Kotoka. Several high-ranking officers, among them the Commander of the Navy, Rear-Admiral D. A. Hansen, and Major-General C. C. Bruce were posted abroad. Other officers were removed from active command and given other work. For example, Brigadier A. A. Crabbe, Commander of the First Infantry Brigade, was appointed Chairman of the Central Region Committee of Administration.

A military regime which can place no reliance on the loyalty of its armed forces, and which has been compelled to imprison or dismiss considerable numbers of its own officers and men, cannot survive. Its very foundations are unsafe. In addition, the position for the "N.L.C." has been complicated right from the start by deep cleavages between Army and Police and by tribal animosities. After Lt. Arthur's bold attempt to overthrow the "N.L.C.", policemen have been instructed to spy on the Army and to report all troop movements to Police Headquarters.

But for a certain lack of co-ordination Arthur's attempt might have ended "N.L.C." rule decisively on 17th April. As it was, the attempted counter-coup presented the most serious challenge the regime had so far had to face. In fact, it has never recovered. The original "N.L.C." no longer exists.

The leaders of the attempted counter-coup Lt. Arthur, Lt. Moses Yeboah and 2nd Lt. Ebenezer Osei Poku, were tried by a 5-man military tribunal. In the course of the trial they fearlessly gave the reasons for their action, stating that the "N.L.C." had no political mandate, that members of the "N.L.C." were amassing private fortunes, and that they were deeply dissatisfied with the way the "N.L.C." was governing the country. Lt. Arthur told the tribunal that those who carried out the military and police action of 24th February 1966 had done precisely what he himself had tried to do; that is, to overthrow the government by force. The only difference between the two "coups" was that the 24th February one had been successful and his had failed. Steadfastly, the prisoners refused to implicate any other army officers or civilians. Lt. Arthur accepted full responsibility himself and declared that he was prepared to face the consequences of failure. He did not consider, however, that his action had failed completely, since it had demonstrated the weakness of the "N.L.C." and the existence of deep dissatisfaction among Ghanaians. It had, he said, "set people thinking".

Lt. Arthur and Lt. Yeboah were sentenced to death by firing squad, and 2nd Lt. Osei Poku to 30 years imprisonment with hard labour. With appalling barbarism which shocked the world the execution took place in public at 9 a.m. on the 9th of May at the army firing range at Teshie, where a special enclosure was erected for spectators. The heroism of these two young officers will never be forgotten. As they stepped from the helicopter which brought them to the place of execution they waved to the waiting crowd, which roared back in acknowledgement. Fearing that the situation might get out of control the two men were quickly hidden from view until the time for execution. They were then led out to the stakes, Lt. Arthur with his eyes uncovered, having refused to be blindfolded. Both men fell quickly at the first burst of fire, but it seems Lt. Arthur did not die immediately, and the firing squad was ordered to fire an extra volley into his body.

The courage shown by Lts. Arthur and Yeboah is rare, and of the highest quality. They did not die in vain. Their example has provided inspiration for patriots throughout our continent, and set a standard of energy and sacrifice unsurpassed in the long history of revolutionary struggle.

The following Situation Reports reveal some of the immediate aftermath:

21.4.67

From Inspector General/Police/Accra to Police/all Regions. Following signal from Army Headquarters is quoted for your information and compliance. Quote— Troop movements. It is urgently requested that from today you keep this headquarters informed of all troops movements in all regions at all times. Unquote. Acknowledge.

21.4.67

From Police/Brong Ahafo Region to Insp. Gen/Police/ Accra. Information received that certain chiefs and people in villages and towns in Brong Ahafo region jubilating in favour of the failure of the counter coup with unfavourable expressions. The regional committee of administration met and directed investigations and questioning of those affected, majority being ex-C.P.P. activists and chiefs. Full report follows.

22.4.67

From Police/West Region to Insp. Gen/Police/Accra. During the abortive coup of 17.4.67 certain proscribed C.P.P. elements were alleged to have jubilated openly, and meted out certain statements hailing Nkrumah's return. Presently twenty-two persons including five women have been taken into custody at Sekondi. Please advise as so many cases all over the region.

27.4.67

From Insp. Gen/Police/Accra to All Regional Commanders. During the night of 26.4.67, thieves broke into customs magazine at James Town and stole quantity of arms and ammunition. Alert all men and road blocks within your area to search vehicles diligently for stolen arms and ammunition. Report by signal result of search to this Headquarters by 01.00 hours each day until further notice. Acknowledge.

28.4.67

From Insp. Gen./Police/Accra to all Regional Commanders. All vulnerable points as for internal security scheme will be manned forthwith 24 hours round the clock. These should include Broadcasting Department, Installations, Telephone Exchanges, Post and Telegraphic Installations, Magazines, Ferries and Government Transport Yards. With regards to bridges special importance to be placed on lower Adomi near Akosombo and Beposo in Western Region. Forward list of points manned in your areas, stating Police and Army strength.

17.5.67

From Special Branch/Northern Region to Special Branch /Kumasi. Grateful confirm if Alhaji Ware Grumah, Alhadji Abu, Alhadji Halidu Damuege, Alhadji Abdulai and Mallam Midzim Waya now hiding at Salaga are wanted for jubilating during the recent military insurrection. All are members of the defunct C.P.P.

Soon after the attempted counter-coup, the "N.L.C." announced that Accra airport was to be named Kotoka Airport, and that a Trust Fund was to be established. How contributions were obtained is shown in the signal sent by Harlley, on 23rd May, to all police stations:

Inspector General/Police directs organise following contribution for Kotoka Trust Fund. District Officers will collect at source payable as follows and forward per special runner to reach this office not later than 10.6.67.

(1) Supt. of Police and Deputy Supt. of Police ...   NC.2.50
(2) Asst. Supt. of Police NC.2.00
(3) Inspector, R.S.M. and District S.M. NC.1.00
(4) All N.C.O.s   ...   .   50NP.
(5) All Constables   ...   .   40NP.

District, Unit Officers will ensure that total amount collected tallies with strength of each district/unit. Members of the public should be encouraged to subscribe to the fund.

On 29th May, 1967, three more men, two civilians and an army officer were sentenced to death by a military tribunal for allegedly conspiring to commit subversion. They were Samson Baffour Awuah, John Osei Poku and Lieutenant Augusuts Owusa Gyimah. A fourth defendant, schoolboy Kofi Owusa, was sentenced to 25 years' imprisonment for failing to report the plot to the authorities. This time, the "N.L.C." thought it wiser to commute the death sentences to long terms of imprisonment. The plot, it was said, had no connection with the attempt of 17th April to overthrow the "N.L.C."

The daily Situation Reports I receive are supplemented by information from intercepted messages between sections of the Army and Police, and by communications, verbal and otherwise, from individuals acting independently. I know in Conakry, within minutes, practically every move made by the "N.L.C." and their supporters, and what is said in their most confidential discussions.

For a time, the "N.L.C." tried to prevent news of the mounting opposition from leaking out, particularly in the foreign press. But as the incidents rapidly increased and became more serious, it became impossible to conceal the fact

129

that widespread opposition was being encountered, and that dangerous rifts were appearing within its own ranks. The setting up of military tribunals to try civilians for so-called "acts of subversion"—a drastic measure involving death by firing squad, or a minimum sentence of 25 years' had labour, without appeal—indicates near panic on the part of the "N.L.C."

In a statement made at a Press Conference held on 22nd February 1967, the "N.L.C." tried to explain why it had become necessary "to tighten security measures in the country". In an attempt to make it appear that the trouble came from outside, I was accused of "subversive activities against Ghana", and the Soviet Union, China and Cuba were attacked for allegedly supporting me with money and arms; though even here, the "N.L.C." seemed unclear of its own argument when it was added: "It may interest you to know, ladies and gentlemen, that most of the explosives are of Communist origin while others are American. The different makes are perhaps meant to create doubt as to who is supporting Kwame Nkrumah." The jittery statement ended: "The public is called upon to be vigilant and to look out for the remaining terrorists who are still at large. A bomb is not selective. It is as much for you as for me."

A similar admission of widespread opposition appeared in an editorial of the *Ghanaian Times* entitled "This Minority is Dangerous". Here again, difficulty was experienced in reconciling the claim of insignificant numbers with the severity of the measures put into operation against them, and the obviously serious view taken of this "minority" by the "N.L.C." In the words of the editorial:

> Let no one be deceived by the words VERY SMALL MINORITY. That small minority is the most influential, the most silent but, paradoxically, the most articulate, the most resourceful and the most strategically-placed group in the community. That small minority can be ten, twenty or even just a hundred, but it has the strength of a thousand because it has the money, it has the devilish machinery for mass propaganda and mass persuasion. It is small but it is strong.
>
> That small minority cannot be easily brushed aside as something capable of just initiating incipient action

which can be nipped in the bud when it is discovered. One thing which we must never forget is that the banned C.P.P. had the most efficient organisation this country has ever known. They had the most fanatical functionaries and activists it had been our misfortune to harbour in the political system of our nation. It had everything the Devil can invent or improvise to suit the shifting situations of political expediency.

SMALL MINORITY indeed! We venture to say that small minority is dangerous.

In March 1967, the "N.L.C.," panic-stricken at the mounting opposition, went to the length of sending 12 Ewes, all of them illiterate criminals taken from the jails of Ghana, to kidnap me and bring me to Ghana "dead or alive". The men were discovered, with two Europeans, aboard a fishing trawler intercepted off the Guinea coast.

Ghanaians have awakened to a full realisation of the deception and betrayal they have suffered since 24th February 1966. They have been able to compare conditions under my government with conditions under the "N.L.C." The experience has strengthened their determination to overthrow the "N.L.C." and to fight against imperialism and neo-colonialism.

8

REPERCUSSIONS

The position of the "N.L.C.", always precarious, has been made even more shaky by the attitude of the progressive independent states of Africa, and the exposure of the so-called "coup" as counter-revolutionary and reactionary.

As soon as the army and police traitors seized power in my absence from Ghana, repercussions in the rest of Africa, and overseas, showed that there was a full awareness of the underlying political implications. Through all the smoke-screen of lies and propaganda, the action was clearly recognised as a blow struck by imperialists ond neo-colonialists and their agents against socialism and the African Revolution. The taking sides "for" and "against" showed once again the familiar groupings of—on the one side, those who are struggling to achieve socialism and the total liberation and unity of the African continent, and on the other, those who want to maintain the status quo, and are fighting a desperate rearguard action to halt the liberation movement.

Both sides have regarded Ghana as a key factor in the struggle. Since independence, Ghana has thrown herself freely and boldly into the struggle for African emancipation. We have proclaimed our firm stand against imperialism, colonialism and neo-colonialism. We have unflinchingly stated that the independence of Ghana is meaningless unless it is linked up with the total liberation of the African continent.

Before 24th February 1966, Ghana was a haven to which the oppressed from all parts of Africa could come to carry on their struggle. Freedom fighters and political refugees from South Africa, Rhodesia, Mozambique, Angola, so-called Portuguese Guinea, the Cape Verde Islands, and other oppressed colonial areas, were given hospitality and encouragement amongst us. Ghana was to them a symbol of hope and an inspiration. It was a centre where they could meet to discuss common problems, and where they could organise and train.

I have never envisaged Ghana in isolation from the rest of Africa. However, it was not until after the events of 24th February 1966 that I realised just how much Ghana also meant to people of African descent living in the U.S.A., the Caribbean, Britain and elsewhere. Messages and letters pour in to me in Conakry showing that they identify their own struggle with the African Revolution. For them, Ghana was symbolic of African liberation and achievement. They felt the blow struck against the Ghanaian people as a personal stab in the back.

To judge from the messages and letters received from men and women of non-African descent all over the world, it appears that the Ghanaian experience is also being felt keenly by the poor and oppressed everywhere. I would like to publish all the letters and messages sent to me. They would be an eye-opener to many.

But I can only quote from a few.

The following cables are representative of many I received from student organisations overseas. They illustrate the view taken of the military and police action in Ghana:

> The African Students' Union in the Netherlands are resolutely in support of the restoration of President Nkrumah and his leadership along the socialist path of development.
>
> We are determined not to rest until our true African freedom fighter President Nkrumah is back in power in Ghana. We cannot tolerate the neo-colonialist plot to undermine the realisation of a Union Government of Africa.
>
> *Paul Adhu Awiti,*
> The Hague, Netherlands.

> We affirm our unreserved faith and confidence in what you have done and still stand for, and strongly condemn the imperialist-organised coup against your government. Victory will be yours.
>
> *Brimah Conteh,*
> President, Africa Society,
> London School of Economics
> and Political Science,
> London, W.C.2.

133

Statement made by the Federation of African Students in the Soviet Union:

The Federation considers the military coup d'état which took place on February 24th 1966, in Ghana as a serious blow delivered by the imperialists and their flunkeys against not only the people of Ghana but the fighting peoples of the rest of Africa.

Dr. Kwame Nkrumah, as President of Ghana, is fighting at the forefront of the struggle for freedom and African unity. The coup against his regime cannot be understood in any other way than that the forces of the world imperialist system, together with their agents on the continent of Africa, have decided to destroy the strong anti-imperialist front that has been built by Kwame Nkrumah together with other eminent leaders of our peoples.

We are categorically opposed to the coup d'état. We call upon the people of Africa to be alert against further attempts on our freedom and unity. We therefore support the stand taken by Guinea, Mali, Congo (Brazzaville) and other progressive governments on the Ghana affair.

We regard the peoples of Africa as the decisive factors of historical development on the continent. The people of Ghana, constituting a part of the African peoples, are the decisive force of development in Ghana itself. And the military rule engineered by the imperialists is bound to crumble down one day if the people of Ghana do not support it.

History has proved that any regime not set up by the people is bound to fall. The victory of the imperialists in Ghana is only temporary. The struggle is still going on. We have a bright future ahead. But before we reach it we shall have to suffer. Our unity in battle will determine the course of history.

We call upon the youth of Africa to close their ranks in support of the people of Ghana and in support of all the people fighting against imperialism and colonialism in all its forms.

134

Long live the freedom struggle of the African people. Long live the valiant people of Ghana led by Kwame Nkrumah, true son of Africa.

Picho Ali,
Secretary General, F.A.S.S.U.,
Moscow, U.S.S.R.

A South African freedom fighter's view is contained in the following quotation from a newsletter of the African People's Democratic Union of South Africa (A.P.D.U.S.A.) published in Lusaka:

The coup d'état staged by the army in Ghana represents a setback in the fight against imperialism in Africa. Kwame Nkrumah is the embodiment of the hopes and aspirations of enslaved Africa for political independence and liberation from the economic shackles of imperialism. Perhaps more than any other leader among the independent states of Africa, he realises that the fight for liberation from colonialism is in fact, a fight against the economic plunder of the continent by imperialist powers.

One further quotation—this time an Arab comment. It comes from the editorial of the *Arab Observer,* a weekly news magazine published in Cairo:

The overall plan of imperialism has now unfolded: to undermine the development of Africa on socialist lines. If at one stage the imperialists were ready to accept an independent Africa it was on one condition: that it would become the projection of their own political image. They wanted Africa to embrace their institutions, capitalism, the multi-party system and all that goes with them. But Africa has chosen otherwise. As President Nyerere once put it, the existence of many parties means the existence of many group interests. But in Africa now there is one interest only, national unity and social justice. The socialist process has started in Africa. What is more, is has developed and become deeply ingrained in the people.

*   *   *

The genuine African revolution has identified itself with socialism . . . . A systematic process was initiated by the neo-colonialists aiming at isolating the non-capitalist countries of Africa—Ghana, Guinea, Mali, Congo (Brazzaville), Tanzania and the U.A.R. In their efforts to do this, the imperialists and neo-colonialists reverted even to the old power politics game. They began a process of political counter-pointing, aiming at the creation of new groupings and new pacts. They also began to create new interest groups or to strengthen already-existing ones. They concentrated their efforts on the armies. Their new pattern for Africa—their counter revolution has become military.

The reaction of the enemies of the African Revolution to events in Ghana on 24th February 1966, may be summed up in the brief report of a newspaper correspondent in Salisbury, Rhodesia:

Spirits Highest Since U.D.I.

The coup against Dr. Nkrumah in Ghana has raised spirits in Rhodesia higher than since the declaration of independence on November 11th (1965).

They had every reason to celebrate. It was quite clear that a severe blow had been struck against the liberation and unity movement in Africa. Moreover, the Ghana situation had caused the shelving of the Rhodesian issue by the Ministerial Council of the Organisation of African Unity (O.A.U.). The O.A.U. Foreign Ministers met at the beginning of March 1966 in Addis Ababa to discuss the question of Rhodesia and to plan joint action, but when a delegation arrived to represent the military regime in Ghana, the delegations of Guinea, Mali, Tanzania and Egypt walked out in protest. Shortly afterwards, the Zambian, Algerian and Somali delegations also left, and the meeting broke up without achieving anything.

President Nyerere of Tanzania, holding a press conference in Dar-es-Salaam at about this time, asked: "What is happening in Africa? What are the coups about?" He continued:

The last few months have seen changes of governments in many African countries. The latest has been in Ghana. What is behind all this? . . . . Are these revolutions to remove humiliation and oppression in Africa? Let us take the latest in Ghana.

The enemies of Africa are now jubilant. There is

jubilation in Salisbury and Johannesburg. Even a fool could begin to wonder whether the revolutions would help Africa. What was Kwame trying to do? He stood for the liberation of Africa. There is not a single leader in Africa more committed to this than Kwame. Whom did he anger with this commitment to freedom? Certainly not Africa.

He was not annoying Africa in his commitment to the liberation of Africa. He was committed to true independence. He was not merely against ordinary colonialism, he was against neo-colonialism—against a colonial power going out through the political door and coming back and controlling the country through the economic door.

Popular meetings of protest were held in Guinea, Mali, Congo (Brazzaville), Egypt, Senegal and elsewhere. In Ethiopia and Liberia, official statements deplored the turn of events. Ousmane Ba, the Mali Foreign Minister, said that my revolutionary work could not be replaced, and added: "We do not accept that some musical comedy general, helped by policemen, should question the Ghanaian people's twenty years of struggle."

At a Press Conference in Kampala, on 23rd February 1967, President Obote of Uganda said that events in Ghana had opened the eyes of "thinking Africa". A military government had been established "for no reason at all, except that the President was working for the masses in Ghana". He continued: "The military government of Ghana is being praised for having ousted a very capable African in government, a great leader in African unity, a great leader in African integrity, a great leader in Africa, being seen as an *African* and not just as a replica of the Western world or the Eastern world."

As expected, Britain, the United States, West Germany and Israel were quick to give official recognition to the "N.L.C." On the day they recognised the new regime, 4th March, only four African states had recognised it. However, others fell into line once the lead had been given. Some African states have since given de facto recognition, but others, for example, Guinea, Zambia and Tanzania, have had nothing to do with the military junta.

Within the first few days, the "N.L.C." launched an attack on all persons and organisations connected in any way with the Pan-African movement. The Bureau of African Affairs and the African Affairs Centre in Accra were immediately closed down. The former, founded in 1960, was established for the study of developments in other parts of Africa, and to further the activities of all organisations working for the freedom and unity of Africa. The African Affairs Centre, opened in 1959, housed freedom fighters from all over Africa.

Spark, L'Etincelle, Voice of Africa, Freedom Fighters Weekly, Pan-Africanist Review, African Chronicler, and the *Bulletin on African Affairs,* all periodicals published by the Bureau of African Affairs, were banned. and editors and reporters flung into prison.

The headquarters of the All-African Trade Union Federation (A.A.T.U.F.) was closed down. The Secretariat of A.A.T.U.F. had summoned all African workers to get mobilised against what it termed "the new pro-imperialist puppet regime", and called on them "to give an indispensable support to the workers and people of Ghana and their great leader President Kwame Nkrumah in their struggle to free Ghana from the grip of reactionary neo-colonialism and imperialism". The "N.L.C." dismissed all loyal T.U.C. officials and set up a puppet T.U.C. which disaffiliated from A.A.T.U.F.

The brilliant African scholar, Dr. W. Alphaeus Hunton, whom I had brought to Ghana to be secretary of the Encyclopaedia Africana project was deported. My object, when I inaugurated the project, was to produce and publish an All-African Encyclopaedia containing in its many volumes detailed and up-to-date information on all aspects of the life and culture, thought and resources of our great continent. The idea had been proposed as long ago as 1909 by Dr. W. E. B. Du Bois, but for over 50 years he could not get support for the idea. In his extreme old age he came to Ghana at my invitation in order to spend his last years there and to devote himself to the preparatory work for the Encyclopaedia. The "N.L.C." pretend to be continuing to produce the Encyclopaedia Africana but they have scattered the records upon which it was to be based and dismissed most of the staff engaged on the project and abandoned the principle and ideology which inspired it.

Other organisations of a Pan-African character were either closed down, or found it impossible to continue in the counter-revolutionary, reactionary atmosphere of "N.L.C." Ghana.

But probably the most disgraceful part of the "N.L.C.'s" attack on the liberation and unity movement was its treatment of African freedom fighters and political refugees. As soon as the "coup" took place, many of them fled from Ghana, knowing what to expect from a clique of military and police traitors. But hundreds were unable to leave in time. Men like Juan-Martin Tchaptchet and Michael N'Doh of the Union des Populations du Cameroun (U.P.C.), and Potlake K. Leballo, Acting President of the Pan-Africanist Congress (P.A.C.) were arrested and imprisoned, together with many more who had come to Ghana seeking refuge and help. They were abused and humiliated by soldiers and police. Matthew Nkoana, a South African, was dragged out of hospital at gun point though he was still a sick man. He writes:

> " I was allowed no time to wash or to have breakfast which had been served. A soldier who said I was too slow putting on my clothes ordered me to carry my shoes and walk barefoot through the corridors and the hospital yard to their car—all in the full view of hospital staff and patients.
>
> "As I walked along I was slapped on the right side of the neck by a young soldier who said I should walk faster. At no time was I told why this treatment was being meted to me, or what their interest in me was, but I was harshly ordered about amidst threats of violence."

At the request of certain puppet and colonial governments, numbers of political refugees and freedom fighters were bundled on to planes and sent back to their countries of origin, where several of them faced a death sentence. An eminent Nigerian professor from the Ideological Institute in Winneba, after being badly beaten and held in prison for several weeks, was sewed in a sack and dragged across the airport tarmac before being tossed into the baggage compartment of an aircraft bound for Lagos.

The "N.L.C." went on to close down the training camps for freedom fighters in Ghana, and to expose them to the glare of world publicity. Foreign correspondents were taken on conducted tours and allowed to take photographs. Descriptions of weapons and equipment, and plans of the camps, were later published in a pamphlet issued by the "N.L.C." in a pathetic attempt to make it appear that the camps had been set up for the subversion of independent African states. But the attempt misfired badly, and its only effect was to bring the "N.L.C." into even greater contempt.

I set up the training camps in Ghana with the co-operation of freedom fighters from all over Africa. Their purpose was to provide training for those intending to win freedom for Africans in Rhodesia, Angola, Mozambique, South Africa, so-called Portuguese Guinea, the Cape Verde Islands, and in South West Africa. Yet these were the camps closed down by the "N.L.C." and exposed to imperialists. The dishonesty, deception and treachery of the "N.L.C.'s" pledge of support for the liberation movement, made four days after they seized power, is glaringly apparent.

Ghana's prestige has never been so low as it is now, after over a year of "N.L.C." misrule. The voice of Ghana formerly carried some weight in Africa, at the United Nations and elsewhere. Now it counts for nothing. It merely swells the chorus of third-rate, puppet states who slavishly echo the imperialist and neo-colonialist line.

Close links were forged with these states as soon as the "N.L.C." was formed. So-called "missions of goodwill" were hastily despatched to them, and to various client states which had been established by neo-colonialists and their agents, as a *cordon sanitaire* around progressive Ghana.

However, even these like-minded friends of the "N.L.C." have been shocked by some of the actions of the army and police clique. There has been the filthy smear campaign, the savage treatment of loyal and respected Ghanaian citizens, the clamping down on all political activity, the spreading of lies such as the one that I had resigned my position as constitutional head of state, the setting up of military tribunals and firing squads—and then of course, the infamous arrest of Guinea's foreign minister and 18 other officials in a Pan-American plane at Accra Airport on 29th October 1966, when they were en route to an O.A.U. meeting in Addis Ababa.

This latter episode, perhaps more than any other, brought home to all but the deliberately blind the true nature of the

140

military-police seizure of power in Ghana. The "N.L.C.," by arresting the Guinean delegation, hoped to force Guinea to send back to Ghana the 81 Ghanaians who were with me in Conakry, whom they asserted were being held there against their will. President Sékou Touré immediately rejected the "N.L.C." claim, and condemned American complicity in the the plot. He ordered all Americans out of the country, closed the office of Pan-American Airways, and declined to attend the O.A.U. Conference while the "N.L.C." delegation sat there representing Ghana.

At the O.A.U. meeting, the delegation from Ghana was treated with utter contempt. Every time one of them tried to speak, delegates made a noise so that he could not be heard. Eventually, the "N.L.C." was compelled to agree to the release of the Guinean diplomats, and a 3-man O.A.U. mission was sent to Conakry to interview my Ghanaian entourage. The mission interviewed each of the Ghanaians separately and privately. They were told that they could immediately board the aircraft waiting at Conakry airport and be escorted back by the O.A.U. mission under a safe conduct agreement. Every one of them refused the offer, and personally signed a statement to this effect. In addition, the Ghanaians called a meeting, passed and signed a resolution of protest, and drafted an open letter to the "N.L.C." which they all signed.

The open letter to the "N.L.C." follows:

> We have been rather embarrassed and certainly extremely annoyed to learn that your clique has arrested and detained four Guinean diplomats (including the Foreign Minister) and fifteen Guinean students who were in transit at Accra International Airport on October 29, 1966. We understand you to have declared then that your action was because we, the Ghanaian entourage of Osagyefo here in Conakry, were being detained here against our will. In view of this allegation, we are forced to communicate very reluctantly with you.

> We have been interested to note your apparent concern for our welfare inherent in your declaration, but we are far from deceived by it.

> We observe that since your neo-colonialist rebellion

141

of February 24 this year, your relentless witch-hunt for progressive Ghanaians has shocked freedom lovers everywhere. We are mindful that the most victimised people in this vendetta are our comrades of the Presidential Detail Department whom we left at home. We are cognisant that even today—nine months after your treachery—you still hunt for those of the Presidential Detail Department whom you have so far failed to put behind bars. To mention only a few examples:

(a) As recently as October 28, Comrade Samuel Amalamah was illegally arrested at Tarkwa (in the Western Region) and imprisoned in Sekondi also in the Western Region.

(b) Police and Special Branch spies are even now combing the Western Region in a hunt for Comrade R. B. Assyne who is believed to have sought refuge in the Region.

We could enumerate many other examples. However, it suffices us to add only that your clique has even published and circulated material on all of us in Conakry with Osagyefo the President in which we are described as "wanted persons".

That is why we find your apparent concern for us not only surprising but also totally contradictory. Indeed, the deliberate dishonesty and duplicity inherent in this "concern" is completely belied by the sadistic inhumanity your clique has always ladled out with such enthusiasm. This is why we do not hesitate to reiterate our conviction that your clique is a notorious liars' council.

We suggest here that in the unlikely event that your clique has at last developed a semblance of conscience and is minded to make a redress of some of the many evils it has perpetrated, you might consider releasing from so-called "protective custody" the thousands of innocent Ghanaians you have detained. It is so pointless and hypocritical to arrest nineteen people (including a diplomatic delegation) in demand for the release of about one hundred people when you already hold so many in arbitrary detention.

Since you declare that your scandalous arrest and detention of the 19 Guinean nationals including the diplomats was because of our forceful detention here in Guinea, we have passed a resolution denying our alleged detention. In it we have also declared our attitude to your clique and your action. We are sending a copy of this resolution to you for your information.

We would like to emphasise to you, that your allegation that we are here under any form of detention is a mistake. We observe that the genuineness of this mistake demands an almost impossible ignorance about our situation here in Conakry, where our liberty and happiness is no secret at all. We contend that your allegation is a deliberate lie, concocted by you for the purpose of your own scandalous actions. You might note our very strong protest against your usage of our name in connection with your perpetration of any such scandalous acts and mockery of international law.

We anticipate your insistence on the genuineness of the mistake in your allegation. In this event we can only suggest that you seriously consider changing your sources of information. Further, we undertake here, quite apart from sending you a copy of our resolution, to tell you what you should have known long ago.

1. We are here in Guinea not under any suppression, promise, duress, or threat. Each one of us is here by voluntary choice springing from a conviction of the justness of our cause. Far from being under any form of detention, all of us here are quite happy and totally free.

2. We remind you that up to this very day, there has been no constitutional change of government in Ghana. Hence, we, as you also should be, are aware of and owe allegiance to only that constitutional Government of Ghana, spear-headed by the Convention People's Party and under the able, wise and progressive leadership of Osagyefo President Kwame Nkrumah.

3. We consider your regime as a mere clique set up by a handful of rebellious army and police officers and

therefore illegitimate and unconstitutional. To us, and to all progressive people, your clique is an offspring of a neo-colonialist intrigue which is doomed to failure by the very decadence of both its architects and executors.

4. We have been very amused to see your so-called amnesty to us. Please, make no mistake here! If without us you cannot run the country whose administration you have temporarily stolen by force of arms, then it is just too bad. Because as long as you have anything to do with the administration of the country, we are not coming back to Ghana unless it means your elimination.

We will never be willingly prepared to serve under or have anything (your elimination excluded) to do with your clique of usurpers from the parade grounds who are not only systematically selling our country, but are also enthusiastically destroying the achievements others have done so much to make possible. Unlike you and others, we are not prepared to betray our country and our people. We are not prepared to become traitors. We are not cowards. We understand and appreciate the cause which we are following and we have the courage of our convictions. For the cause of Socialist Ghana and for the greater African Revolution we shall always be prepared to go to any lengths. This is why we are prepared to follow wherever Osagyefo President Kwame Nkrumah leads! This is why we are here in Conakry in the Republic of Guinea! Such is our stand.

Long live Osagyefo President Kwame Nkrumah;
Long live Socialist Ghana;
Long live the Progressive People of Ghana;
Long live the Revolutionary Movement for African Unity;
Long live all Freedom Fighters."

The following is the resolution passed at the meeting held by my Ghanaian entourage in Conakry:

We Ghanaians who have accompanied Osagyefo President Kwame Nkrumah to Conakry in the Republic of Guinea, have been very disturbed by the news that the self-styled "National Liberation Council" in Ghana has arrested four Guinean diplomats en route to Addis Ababa, and 15 Guinean students en route to Nigeria.

We are even more disturbed to learn that the so-called "N.L.C." has taken this action because "about 100 Ghanaians are being detained in Guinea against their will".

We assume that the Ghanaians concerned in this ridiculous allegation are we who constitute the entourage of Osagyefo President Kwame Nkrumah here in Guinea. On this assumption we the above mentioned Ghanaians severally and collectively solemnly resolve that:

1. We are satisfied that on 24th February 1966, a neo-colonialist imperialist instigated rebellion was executed in Ghana by a handful of decadent army and police officers who now style themselves the "National Liberation Council".

   We declare that we do not recognise the so-called "National Liberation Council" as a Government in Ghana. For us and indeed for all true Ghanaians free from the threat of guns, bayonets and "protective custody". the so-called "National Liberation Council" is no more than a clique of four soldiers and four policemen who represent only themselves and the interests of neo-colonialist imperialism.

2. We maintain that for us, as true Ghanaians, Osagyefo Dr. Kwame Nkrumah is still the constitutional head of Ghana. We have followed him willingly to Guinea, we are happy of the honour to serve him through thick and thin, and, if such should be necessary, we shall always be prepared to lay down our lives for him and for a Ghana truly free from neo-colonialist oppressors and their stooges.

3. We strongly deny the allegation that we are here in Conakry in the Republic of Guinea under any form of duress, threat or promise. We are here in Guinea by our own free choice and we are totally free and happy here.

145

We demand the immediate and public withdrawal by the "N.L.C." of this baseless allegation.

4. We strongly and angrily condemn the "N.L.C.'s" arrest and detention of 19 Guinean nationals including Guinea's Foreign Minister. We declare that the action is baseless and irresponsibly provocative of a situation tending to threaten peace not only in Africa but also in the world at large.

We denounce it as one of the imperialist intrigues hatched in collusion with their stooges for the destruction of the fabric on which the organisation of African Unity is woven.

5. We take strong objection to the "N.L.C's" usage of our names in the perpetration of such a scandalous flouting of international law. In this respect we are undertaking to send a strong open letter of protest to the so-called "N.L.C." in Ghana.

6. We demand the immediate release, with due apologies, of the 4 Guinean diplomats and 15 Guinean students who have been so wrongfully arrested by the so-called "N.L.C." in our name.

7. We maintain that we are not prepared to go to Ghana where the traitorous "N.L.C." has even the remotest control. We emphatically refuse to serve under, or have anything to do with cowardly usurpers, stooges and renegades who are shamelessly prepared to sell their own country and kin to neocolonialist imperialists."

As President Nyerere said, on his way home from the O.A.U. conference in November 1966: "Africa is in a mess."

The O.A.U. has been rendered ineffective, many nominally independent states have puppet regimes, and large areas of our continent remain unliberated. This will be the case so long as we remain disunited and fail to establish a Union Government of Africa. But I was sad when I read the comment of a Nigerian correspondent on the position "N.L.C." Ghana occupies in the minds of progressive Africans: "Ghana," he said, "makes me and Africa ashamed."

9

IN CONAKRY

Conakry is magnificently situated on a promontory of land jutting into the sea. Wherever you go in the city, you are only a few minutes away from sandy beaches and beautiful views of neighbouring coasts. Off-shore are several islands, Kassa, Fotoba, Tamara and others, one of which is said to have provided the inspiration for Robert Louis Stevenson's *Treasure Island*.

During the last ten months I have received numerous cables, telephone calls and letters from reporters and members of broadcasting and television companies asking permission to visit me in Conakry. They are apparently interested to know what I am doing and what I think about recent political developments in Africa and elsewhere. I have declined all offers of interviews, since they could serve no useful purpose. Genuine supporters of the African Revolution know my political views and the stand I have taken.

President Sékou Touré, the Political Bureau of the Guinea Democratic Party, and the people of Guinea have made me feel completely at home; and I shall always look back on the months I spent with them as among the happiest in my life. I have been able to do so many things I longed to do but never had the time. I have been able to read as much as I like, to study the latest books on politics, history, literature, science and philosophy, to step up my writing, to reflect, and to prepare myself physically and mentally for the militant phase of the revolutionary struggle. I have played a lot of tennis; and have gone for long brisk walks, covering several miles at a time. I have had daily lessons in French from Madame Julienne Batchily. I have learned to drive. Most days I have found time to play chess, a game I always find stimulating, and at the same time relaxing. Recently, I have undergone a course of military training.

My days have been full, but not with the tedious administrative details of government. It has been a great joy to have time to spend with the many visitors who have come to Guinea to see me from all over Africa, and from countries overseas. These visitors, freedom fighters and members of progressive organisations, have discussed their problems with me. Far from feeling isolated, as the imperialist press would have its readers believe, I have never felt more in touch with African and world affairs. I have an efficient communications system which enables me to keep up to date with events inside Ghana and elsewhere.

The diplomatic representatives in Conakry of various states call on me regularly. I am in daily touch with President Sékou Touré and members of the Guinea Government, who visit me every evening for supper. Madame Andrée Sékou Touré is often present on these occasions. So also are M. Diallo Saifoulaye, Minister of State, Dr. Beauvogui Sansana, Minister of Foreign Affairs, Diallo Abdoulaye, Director of Political Affairs in the Foreign Ministry and Roving Ambassador, and other members of the Guinea government. They have made me feel very welcome. M. Sana Camara, Chief Protocol Officer in charge of my household, and Police Commissioner Abdoulaye Combassa, have constantly sought my comfort and protection. I must mention too, the soldiers and gendarmes who guard my residence, and the many Guineans who carry out other household and office duties.

Each day there is a vast amount of office work to be done. Reports, compiled from radio and other sources, have to be read, analysed and acted upon, correspondence dealt with, and detailed plans made for the carrying on of the revolutionary struggle.

The correspondence alone, and telephone and cable communications, keep my secretaries and myself busy for many hours every day. The messages of support which continue to flow in from all over the world are a great source of encouragement to me personally and to the Ghanaians with me in Conakry. All these men were with me on the Vietnam mission, and they have stayed with me ever since, not once showing any despondency, or doubt about the final outcome of the struggle, and the return of legal government to Ghana. I have been very touched by their loyalty, and have admired the way they have adapted to the life in Conakry, away from their families and in unfamiliar surroundings. They have won the affection and respect of the people of Guinea, who give them a rousing reception every time they appear on state and public occasions.

In November 1966, when the "N.L.C." was holding the O.A.U. Guinea delegation prisoner in Accra, Ghanaians in Conakry joined their Guinean brothers in the great march-past to celebrate Army Day. It effectively gave the lie to the "N.L.C." claim that they were being held in Guinea against their will. The thousands in the packed stadium gave the Ghanaians thunderous applause.

I stood then, as on all state occasions, beside President Sékou Touré. It was the first time I had appeared in public in army uniform, and I was amused when I heard that a foreign diplomat had asked the man next to him: "Who is the parachute officer next to Sékou Touré?" I did not realise what an effective disguise the uniform and beret provided.

Guinea, like Ghana, has immense natural resources, and it has been most interesting to visit the many industrial and agricultural development projects being undertaken all over the country. Guinea is building its economy on a socialist basis, with a strong state sector. Everywhere, I have seen evidence of industrial and agricultural progress being made. I was particularly interested in a visit President Sékou Touré and I paid to a large new textile factory near Conakry which was officially opened in June 1966. There I saw one of the most modern cotton spinning and weaving complexes in Africa, with hundreds of machines.

I have grown extremely fond of Conakry. From the seafront villa where I stay, I can see the hills of Sierra Leone, and in the other direction, the distant shores of so-called Portuguese Guinea, where a fierce liberation struggle is going on. The off-shore islands, the fishing boats, and the bulky merchant ships which come and go from the busy harbour at Conakry, will always be in my mind when I think of the days I spent here. I shall never forget either, the rainy season. How I enjoyed it! Although it can rain heavily for days on end in Ghana, I have never experienced anything like the Guinea storms. When it

149

is cold, and when the rain is crashing down, I am at one with the elements. I have told President Sékou Touré that I would like to visit Guinea every year for the rains.

During the first few months of my stay in Guinea, I broadcast regularly to the people of Ghana over Radio Guinea's "Voice of the Revolution". The purpose of these broadcasts was to inform Ghanaians of the facts about what had taken place in Ghana, and to encourage them to keep up their resistance. The "N.L.C." tried to prevent people listening to the broadcasts, and many radio sets were confiscated. But people listened in secret, gathering round shared radios, and then passing on my messages to those who had been unable to listen. For certain good reasons I eventually stopped broadcasting regularly at specified times, and instead broadcast only on special occasions, or when it became necessary to expose a particularly vicious lie spread by the "N.L.C." A case in point was the lie that I had resigned as President of Ghana. I denied this in a short broadcast made on 5th December 1966. Apparently my broadcasts are heard in many countries other than Ghana. For example, I have received letters from listeners in South Africa, Sierra Leone, Liberia, Gambia and Nigeria —to mention only a few.

Probably the personal and written contacts with members of progressive movements and organisations throughout the world has been the most stimulating and memorable of all my experiences during this transition period. I publish here, three recent letters from African leaders. The first is from Oscar Kambona, who was then Minister of Regional Administration in President Nyerere's cabinet:

> The United Republic of Tanzania,
> Regional Administration,
> P.O. Box 1949,
> Dar-es-Salaam.
>> 18th August 1966

Your Excellency President Kwame Nkrumah,
State House,
Conakry,
Guinea.

Dear Sir,
    I am sorry that I am going to take up your precious

time, but you have always had place in your heart for me so please let me have a few minutes.

I have been very anxious to hear all about you, and I am glad that all the information that I have is that you are well. Thank heavens.

We, the people of Africa, will never forget nor let you down. We know what you have done for Africa. Africans' dignity has something to do with you. For there was no Africa before you came on to the scene. Your losses are temporary, Sir. The stooges will not remain long. The imperialists are working hard with their lies and fabrications. But the true sons and daughters of Africa will never sway to this propaganda. Africa and her true sons and daughters are solidly behind you, Sir. When the hour to strike comes do please let me know so that I may join those who will carry the banner to victory. I am one of those soldiers who are ready to die in the service of Africa.

Imperialists are jubilant with their temporary gain, but they forget that the masses of Africa are stronger. We will march into Accra, and every part of Ghana will be free again. Please, Sir, be patient. Never despair. The path to victory may be long and difficult. But men and women have overcome these difficulties throughout history. So Africa will overcome these losses. The youth in Tanzania and the whole of Africa are awaiting your bugle to sound, and all will be with you in the streets of Accra to destroy the imperialists and their scavengers.

I am enclosing herewith some cuttings from the British imperialist press, and some correspondence for your information. I have decided to give up one-third of my salary to help to pay your expenses in Guinea. I am sending a few pounds* with Ambassador Biro, and will keep on sending some more.

If there is anything you would like me to do, please let me know. I am in the service of Africa.

*A cheque for £490 was enclosed. I decided I would not make use of the money, but would keep it for my return to provide a scholarship for a Tanzanian student to study in one of the Universities of Ghana.

May God and the good spirits of Africa keep you well and healthy. The youth of Africa are solidly behind you. One day you will march triumphantly through the streets of true Accra and Ghana.

> Long live Kwame
> Long live Africa.

> Yours in the service of Africa,
> (Signed) *Oscar Kambona.*

Less than a month after I got the letter from Kambona, I received the following note from Ibrahim A. Farah, President and Founder of the Somali Co-operative Movement, from which I now quote:

> The President,
> Somali Agriculturalists
> Co-operative and Community.
> 10th September 1966

Osagyefo President Kwame Nkrumah,
President of the Republic of Ghana,
Conakry,
Guinea.

Dearest Brother President,

Africa, Asia, Latin America, and all freedom-loving peoples all over the world are mourning for you. The dreadful events which took place during your absence from Ghana in February last, have shocked the world. As a result, the once leading Ghana does not exist any longer in our hearts.

*   *   *

It is a terrible blow against us—we African freedom lovers and ardent followers of your teachings. It is also widely recognised that the coup was also the end of the O.A.U. The imperialists and colonialists are breathing the air of relief after the formation of a puppet government in Ghana, because you have been a thorn in their throat. They (the colonialists) wanted to swallow the whole African continent, blood and bones, but you showed them to their homes in Europe, and you made their "come-back" impossible. Finally, fully convinced of the fact that your whole life was dedicated to the total liberation, the total survival of all mankind, and particularly, for the progress and well-being of the African continent and its peoples—the solution, so far as the colonialists are concerned, was only to find ways and means of subversion, to put a yes-man traitor in your place as Head of State.

The question which every nationalist asks him/herself is: "Is it the end of the African Revolution, or is it just a beginning?" During the last fifteen years, Africa has lost more outstanding leaders and statesmen than Europe and Asia put together. Patrice Lumumba was murdered; Ahmed Ben Bella ousted, and no one knows of his whereabouts, except those concerned; Joshua Nkomo is in the hands of those diabolical white settlers in Rhodesia; and last but most important of all, the great African leader, President Kwame Nkrumah is missing (though only for a temporary period of time).

So far, the colonialists have succeeded in playing with Africa, and the cold war has been shifted to all corners of this continent, which used to be the most peaceful place for man to live in—without disturbance and want. Heavy wounds are inflicted on us, and it seems our recovery is doubted . . . . I vowed to follow to the end any genuine African leader who dedicates his life for the common good, common welfare, common progress, and the total liberation of Africa as a whole. I am very sure of your greatness, President Nkrumah, and I am ready to die for you because I feel that my life is nothing to be compared with yours. You have saved millions of lives, and the peoples of all countries recognise your achievements.

Since that shameful time of February 1966, I and friends of mine in the Somali Republic have been actively collecting information from the Somali masses, and we have been fully assured by thousands that they are ready to serve the great African leader, President Kwame Nkrumah, even at the cost of their lives. I sincerely hope that the President will give us the opportunity to fight for our good future and for the future of all the peoples of our continent.

Our Agricultural Co-operative was facing disaster at the time of the 1961 flood, but you saved us and made it possible for us to exist and face the future by granting us the vitally-needed assistance, which was £3,000. From that day, the peoples of Somalia came to know you better, and also Ghana and Ghanaians. From that day, we understood that you are a genuine African leader, because we arrived just from the "blue", but when we told you about our difficulties, you never doubted us, and you helped us at a time when a person clearly distinguishes between friends and foes.

We thank very much Brother Ahmed Sékou Touré the President of the Republic of Guinea, for his kindness.

Yours for ever in the Service of Africa,
(Signed) *Ibrahim A. Farah (Dagah)*,
President and Founder.

The third is from Oginga Odinga:

My Dear Kwame,

I ardently send you warmest felicitations and new year greetings wishing you a very happy and successful future.

Foremost, I wish to take this opportunity to thank you for writing such a glorious foreword to my book, *Not Yet Uhuru*. Your luminous foreword has become a permanent inspiration that touches my very soul.

Dispite the long distance dividing us, I wish to assure you that I am always with you. I sincerely hope that this year will be one of many successes in the struggle against imperialism headed by the U.S. and its accomplices such as the bloodthirsty gangsters in Ghana who have temporarily reversed the revolutionary force that was begining to thrive in Africa. Although the imperialists with their hired lackeys are still frantically trying to isolate you from your beloved people, to me, this is only temporary.

I am in constant touch with many patriotic Ghanaians who from time to time brief me on the enthusiasm and brilliant victories the Ghana masses are scoring in the war to free Ghana once again from the American accomplices. This fact hardly receives publicity in the imperialist dominated Western papers found here and there in Africa.

The leading enemies of African unity together with degenerated elements have sneaked into our ranks and are causing chaos which would plunge Africa into a more protracted dilemma if we do not act immediately. When I noticed the KANU was in very deep collusion with very dangerous invisible foreign imperialists, I was left with only one alternative to resign and form a more radical and progressive Party (Kenya People's Union—K.P.U.).

KANU has slowly, gradually and eventually fallen into the hands of reactionary forces actively perpetuating foreign economic domination. Fear that many elected members were going to resign from KANU to join KPU led KANU into making new laws designed entirely to protect KANU and the Government from total collapse. Laws hurriedly made require those who resigned from KANU to resign their seats in Parliament in order to recontest them. I along with all the patriotic militant MPs who recontested the seats witnessed the unholy work of invisible masters ruling Kenya today. We were intimidated, some of our supporters were murdered but the assassins were never brought to court of law. Votes were rigged by Government administrative machinery. Leading members of our Party were arrested and detained. Lots of our supporters are exposed to all sorts of cruel suppressive moves by the reactionary Government. But still, and contrary to the invisible masters' expectation, the Kenya masses have become more vigilant and are surely out to deal the enemy a crushing blow to restore their economic, political and social rights which have been sold to the imperialists by KANU Party led by Jomo Kenyatta.

It is my firm belief that whatever the imperialists do in Kenya, in Ghana or in any other part of Africa, the oppressed masses will never yield to the oppressor and their victory is inevitable. I pledge to uphold our old Pan-African ideals and spirit and avail myself to

155

fight the enemies of African unity by all means possible. Frenzied aggressions carried out by imperialists lend no time for speculation. It is time for action and I believe our Party together with sister progressive Parties I know of, can act.

Last but not least, I wish the people of Ghana more victory, particularly in their struggle to liberate their beloved country from the bloodthirsty military puppets. Once again my dear comrade, I look forward to fresh successes on your part and hope to have a lot to talk of when we next meet. Pass my warmest regards to all members of your family, your friends and all the comrades-in-arms around you.

Yours in the struggle,

(signed) A. Oginga Odinga

I will always treasure these, and the hundreds of letters from friends and supporters all over Africa and the world.

But these dark days will pass. Nothing can stop the progress of the African revolutionary struggle. On 24th February 1966 Ghana was forced one step backward. We shall take two forward.

10

CONCLUSION

Two important points emerge clearly from the events of 24th February 1966 in Ghana, and the subsequent months of "N.L.C." betrayal and treachery. First, that independent African states must pursue a policy of all-out socialism if they are to survive. Secondly, that the African revolutionary struggle for total continental liberation and the establishment of an All-African Union Government must now enter a phase of planned, unified and centrally-directed armed struggle. While we remain divided no single progressive independent African state is safe.

For years, I have been warning against the dangers, both open and concealed, which threaten the very foundations of our independence. In speeches, broadcasts and in my books I have exposed the workings of imperialism and neo-colonialism and have shown that the only solution for Africa lies in total liberation and unity. In 1965, with the publication of *Neo-Colonialism—The Last Stage of Imperialism,* I showed how the network of foreign business interests have secured a stranglehold over our economic life. In 1966, in *The Challenge of the Congo* my purpose was to expose the insidious ways in which foreign pressures can operate in an independent state. Shortly before I left for Hanoi, on 21st February 1966, I addressed the National Assembly and spoke about the military coups which had occurred in so many parts of Africa. I said that it was not the duty of the army to rule or govern because it had no political mandate, and its duty was not to seek a political mandate.

Every state emerging from colonialism has to face, sooner or later, the threat to its independence of an alliance between local, reactionary elements and imperialist and neo-colonialist interests. The problem is serious, but not insurmountable, once its true nature is assessed and adequate steps are taken in time to prevent it from becoming deep-rooted.

We must be constantly vigilant. Imperialist intelligence organisations are hard at work in Africa, manipulating political pressures internally and externally within developing, independent states. Evidence of their activities may be seen in the conspiracies, subversions, coups and assassinations hitherto virtually outside our political experience, but in recent years a painful reminder that we are not yet masters in our own house.

Government officials, police and army officers, party leaders, newspaper editors and others have been bribed and blackmailed. Local bourgeois reactionaries, dishonest intellectuals and retrogressive chiefs are being used to subvert progressive governments. The tragedy is, that some African Heads of State are themselves actually aiding and abetting imperialists and neo-colonialists.

In Africa, the resistance of the masses to imperialist aggression grows daily. African freedom and unity have become their watchwords. In that alone lies their fulfilment. The higher the level of a people's political awareness the greater is their understanding of their historical mission. Africa is ripe for armed revolution.

This great upsurge of the African peoples can only be effective if it is organised, and if it is armed. The time is past for half-measures and piecemeal solutions. No compromise is possible while reactionary and counter-revolutionary elements exist in Africa, and while imperialists and neo-colonialists are able to make use of them for their own ends.

For the moment the continent is disunited and powerless in world affairs. The "N.L.C." have broken up the freedom fighters' training camps in Ghana and everywhere their movement has become weakened. African opinion is no longer taken into calculation by the great powers nor are African protests on any matter regarded as of any account. This alone, if there were nothing else, would demonstrate the importance of what the C.P.P. and I attempted in our ten years of power. It is the mark of the permanence of our achievement. It is impossible to put the clock back. Those who conducted the "coup" and their western backers have achieved nothing by merely removing me from authority in

Ghana. Indeed they have achieved the reverse of what they intended. Far from the ideas for which Ghana stood being discredited, they have been proved for all to see as correct and as charting the inevitable path which Africa must follow.

Imperialism and neo-colonialism must be attacked wherever they are operating throughout the world, and protracted people's wars must be fought until victory is achieved.

If for a while the imperialists appear to be gaining ground, we must not be discouraged. For time is on our side. The permanency of the masses is the deciding factor, and no power on earth can prevent its ultimate decisive effect on the revolutionary struggle.

APPENDIX

MESSAGES RECEIVED FROM HEADS OF STATE

Modibo Keita, President, Mali.
25.2.66
(Translation)

I have received your very kind message and I am happy to hear that you are well. Please thank our comrades of the People's Republic of China for this important contribution to Africa's struggle for her liberty and her progress.

Yesterday, the 24th February, we heard of the serious events which took place in Ghana and which do no credit to those who have provoked them.

For us, the authors of the coup d'état have committed an act of high treason.

As you say, this is one phase of the unremitting struggle waged by neo-colonialists and imperialists against Africa which wishes to live in freedom and dignity and in friendship with all people who are peace-loving and who wish to build a just society. All Africans, conscious of the grave dangers posed to our peoples and our continent, should mobilise themselves to bar the way to neo-colonialism and imperialism.

The Malian people consider themselves engaged in this struggle.

For this reason your special envoy, assured in advance of our support and assistance, will be welcome in Mali and the visit which you plan to pay us will soon confirm to you the active solidarity of the leaders and people of Mali for the restoration of legality to Ghana.

Ahmed Sékou Touré, President, Guinea.
(Translation)

The Political Bureau and the Government after a thorough analysis of the African situation, following the seizure of power by the instruments of imperialism, have decided:

1. To organise a national day of solidarity with the Ghanaian people next Sunday. Throughout the length and breadth of the country there will take place popular demonstrations on the theme of anti-imperialism, and,

2. To call on all progressive African countries to hold a special conference and take all adequate measures. We think that the time factor is vital here, since it is important to make a riposte without further delay, by every means. Your immediate presence would be very opportune, it seems to us, and we are therefore impatiently waiting for you.

Gamel Abdel Nasser, President, United Arab Republic.
(Translation)

With feelings of anxiety and shock, we, in the United Arab Republic, have heard of the sad events to which the people of Ghana were exposed and of which you wrote in your letter to me dated 25th February.

I agree with you that the forces of colonialism are always trying to undermine the independence of African states, and to draw them again into spheres of influence in order to continue exploiting their resources and shape their fates.

What has happened in Ghana is actually a part of this imperialist plan. To face colonialism in the African continent requires of us all continuous efforts and a sustained struggle to liberate it from old and neo-colonialism.

The setback that has occurred in Ghana must act as a driving force for all of us to continue the struggle for the consolidation of the independence of African peoples, and their liberation from imperialist forces.

I am sure you know that you are always welcome in the United Arab Republic.

Kim Il Sung, Pyongyang.
1.3.66

(Translation)

I have received your letter. We have been making preparations with immense joy for the friendly visit of your Excellency to our country as President of the Republic of Ghana, which could not be realized to our regret.

We are especially enraged at the reactionary coup d'état

which took place in Ghana at the instigation of the imperialists while your Excellency was visiting a number of countries.

The imperialists engineer similar plots and perpetrate subversive activities against progressive countries everywhere. We resolutely condemn the machinations of the imperialists against the just cause of the peoples for national liberation, independence and progress.

We express our unreserved support to your Excellency's determination to fight for the freedom of Ghana on your return to Africa.

Albert Margai, Prime Minister, Sierra Leone.
4.3.66

I wish to acknowledge receipt of your telegram informing me of recent developments in the Republic of Ghana—news of which came as a real and personal shock to me—during the course of your visit to Peking en route to Hanoi.

I have followed your movements since and it is gratifying to note that you were accorded such an impressive and heroic welcome on arrival at Conakry by our Brother Ahmed and the people of the Republic of Guinea.

Whilst we are conscious of the many and divers forces working in Africa which daily and constantly strive to foil our struggle for the final emancipation of those still subject to colonial rule and our ultimate claims to unity, I have nevertheless formed great hope and fortitude in the courage of your convictions and determined efforts to defy all odds in refusing to accept the results of the recent revolt as a fait accompli.

Please accept, my dear Brother, the assurance of my highest consideration, esteem and prayers for your personal well-being and safety.

Lee Kuan Yew, Prime Minister, Singapore.
11.3.66

I have taken two weeks to compose my thoughts to tell you how disturbed I was at the shocking news of what took place in Accra so soon after we last met.

I visited Ghana twice and I do not believe that political changeover has written finish to the chapter of what has gone before. I do not know what exactly happened nor how things will turn out, but I am sure you know that there are many people who wish Ghana and you all the best. The Ghanaians are a vigorous and lively people and they deserve all the vision and leadership which you strove to give them, to make Ghana into a strong, modern part of an Africa whose unity you have always espoused.

My colleague, Rajaratnam, and I remember your kindness to us and your support for Singapore and would like to express our sympathy for you in your moment of distress.

May what you stand for, a united Africa and a great Ghana, triumph and flourish.

A SELECTION FROM PERSONAL LETTERS

The following letters have been selected from among the vast numbers which I have received from all over the world, during my stay in Conakry. In some cases, it has been necessary to omit the names and addresses of the senders.

Ghanaian, London, N.5, England.

28.2.66

I am . . . . . . ,son of . . . . . . , District Commissioner. For five years I have been a £47 a week postman in London. I am married with one child. I do not need any money from you; I do not need any work from you or the government. But because I have no mean good faith in your Presidentship and your world of politics, I do here this day of 28.2.66 offer myself to be called for training anywhere, any time to FIGHT BACK FOR YOUR SAFE RETURN TO GHANA.

Hoping to get a registered reply as soon as possible.

Nigerian student, London, England.

1.3.66

The news of the take-over of government by some thoughtless and irresponsible elements in your country has come as a great shock and absolute distress. Many of our students over here have never dreamt that such an unfortunate incident could ever occur in a country which you built up and which you have modernised with industries. What has happened is a great blow to Ghana and to Africa as a whole. It is very unreasonable that our fellow Ghanaians have taken that course of action.

I am quite sure that all hopes are not yet dashed into pieces. You should take all possible measures open to crush the rebellion and return to power to save Africa from going back to a "dark continent," to redeem its people from ignorance, disease and colonial mentality. If there is any possible way for me to help or render any service I shall not hesitate to do so. May God assist you to overcome "them." I shall write another letter soon.

Ghanaian student, Alessandria, Italy.
2.3.66

Please excuse me and forgive me for the poor way I am addressing this letter to you, all because of time and fear.

I have been greatly awed and heavy in heart, for the shameful and unpatriotic news I read in the papers about the overthrow of your government, which is of the people and mine.

In view of this mishappening, I advise you as an unknown supporter of yours, and hope you will hesitate to return to Ghana till tensions return to normal. But should you think to return, for one reason or the other, I put myself completely at your honourable disposal, to use me in all ways you think justifiable, to see the wish of the people done, and that is the Government of Ghana, and of Ghanaians restored.

I cannot write more, but think you understand me and my feelings. To conclude I introduce myself to you as an unknown believer in Nkrumaism, who for personal reasons did not think to make myself known to you in Ghana. But now I am in Europe, seeking further laurels in a sporting activity. Hoping you have forgiven me as a father my impolite way of writing this letter. Excuse me, I fervently plead for time is running against me, and I cannot wait any longer. In all, I remain with my warmest greetings to Mrs. Fathia Nkrumah and the children.

A. C. Jordan, Dept. of African Languages and Literature, University of Wisconsin, Madison, Wisconsin.
2.3.66

Only yesterday, one of my colleagues at this University asked me what I thought your next move was going to be. I replied laconically: "If I know Kwame Nkrumah, he is not going to take it lying down."

I leave it to you to imagine therefore how glad, how proud

165

I felt this evening, on hearing it announced over the radio that today you landed on Guinea territory and had a warm reception. Courage!

Mauro Buser, Holbeinstrasse 7, 4051 Basel, Switzerland.

3.3.66

Day by day I follow the course of development of Africa and especially that of your country with attention, because I believe that Africa will bring to humanity an immensity of best renovations in every field of human existence if, of course, there will not be a nuclear war, and as a student of physical science I know very well that all would be destroyed.

But I cannot understand why it was possible, that after about 900 years after Ibn Yasin and Abu Bakr, Ghana is another time subjugated by hot-headed military rabble (I don't like militarism); how was it possible that the army could usurp power behind your back (a detestably insidious action) when you went to China? Am I right if I believe that imperialistic hands of dirty U.S. agitators are behind the matter?

I was delighted when I heard how you and Mr. Sékou Touré (obviously a namesake of famous King Askia the Great whose real name was Muhammed Touré) solved that most difficult situation.

You see I like that spirit very much because in Europe it is in very short supply. Our politicians are like old arteriosclerotic senile men. They never have a good idea. About ten years ago they started, for example, to unite Europe—the result—nothing. But Mr. Nyerere from Tanzania did it with Tanganyika and Zanzibar over night.

That's why I would transform the famous phrase of Karl Marx into:

Nations of Africa assemble yourselves.

I see no reason why Africa has to remain like Europe, like minced meat that grows mouldy. (That is my opinion of the situation in Europe.)

I would be very happy if you would give an answer on the question why so many African countries have become militarised states? But I won't be angry if you cannot tell me why, because I know well that you have to do more important matters at present; I would only be a little sad, because I am

166

very much interested in the actual situation in Africa.

A twenty years' old admirer salutes you most respectfully and please give Sékou Touré my kind regards. (I beg your pardon for my bad English, normally I speak German.)

Bucarest, Rumania.
(Translation)
4.3.66

I want you to know that all the African revolutionary students here support you and will continue to support you against the reaction in Ghana.

I am ready to keep you informed of the situation here and to advise you of the Ghanaian situation in Rumania, after the seizure of power in Ghana by imperialist agents. The Ghanaian ambassador in Rumania has recognised the new regime in Accra.

I am ready to tell you the addresses of Ghanaian students who remain loyal to the government and the ideals of Your Excellency Kwame Nkrumah.

My action cannot be considered interference in the internal affairs of Ghana. I am faced with a regime which supports imperialism and the bourgeoisie, and on the other side I see an African revolutionary regime led by Dr. Kwame Nkrumah.

Action taken against the new regime in Accra is action against imperialism, colonialism and neo-colonialism in Africa. It is not interference when a battle against a common enemy is being waged, but rather co-operation in the struggle.

The young freedom fighters of Cameroon who struggle against neo-colonialism, can support only progressive African governments.

Being convinced that the reaction in Accra will not last for long, please accept, Your Excellency, my African greetings.

Theophilus Artman, 440 Green Heart Street, Mackenzie,
Demerara, Guyana.
4.3.66

I am following closely the events which have taken place in Ghana while President Nkrumah was in Peking, and deplore the puppet regime which is being used by the imperialists to hold back the march of African liberation. Though we are thousands of miles away we are keeping abreast with what is taking place in Africa. I am well pleased with the agreement between you and President Sékou Touré. Since the news we wish you to return to Ghana, but with force to put down the puppet regime. We know how you have built Ghana since independence and we in these parts looked on you not only as leader of Ghana but of Africa as a whole. The imperialists would not like leaders as yourself because they realise you to be the most progressive leader in Africa who want to have unity among the Africans. This makes the imperialists scared, as they want to continue to exploit as in Rhodesia, South Africa and Mozambique. They must not be allowed to succeed. I think you should take all help wherever you can get it. For the West will never help the Africans to liberate themselves. They will fortify the Europeans as they have done in Rhodesia, South Africa and Mozambique. I pray that with God's help your aspirations will be achieved. In conclusion, may I say long live you both. Long live the pan-African movement which will be able to liberate our oppressed brothers

Bathurst, Gambia.

4.3.66

I am writing you this letter in the name of the whole of Africa, and as a son on African soil. I feel that it is the duty of every African, and an obligation to acknowledge in writing in connection with the recent coup in your absence in Ghana.

We not only sympathise with you as a person but with the whole idea of African unity. We also appreciate your efforts which we believe will release the whole of Africa from imperialist suppression. We are daily praying for your success, and we are sure the Almighty will also sympathise with you. I believe that perhaps someone somewhere could do something for Africans but we are also sure that you are the first and foremost to redeem Africa and the African people.

I wish to repeat that the Gambian youth will do everything in our power, and if possible fight alongside with you to achieve your ambitions. I and thousands of Gambians sleep, walk and even at work think of you. Greetings to your host, President Sékou Touré and your colleagues.

Nigerian student, London, S.W.18.
4.3.66

Your Excellency, may the Almighty God bless and be with you in your struggle for the emancipation of the black race and to restore constitutional government to Ghana, which is at present being taken over by imperialist powers.

As a wholesome African born in Nigeria, I am deeply in support of you, Nasser and Nyerere, so much so that I cannot think of any other way to express my appreciation and loyalty to you than to offer my unconditional service to you. I am a student still with one year left for me to complete a post-graduate course. I have a wife with three children. In spite of these responsibilities, I am still prepared to do whatever you wish provided you accept my offer. I shall be ready to be your bodyguard even at the point of death. For I'd rather die for a just cause than live for ever.

Signed by 23 students of Szeged Medical University, Dugonics Ter 13, Szed, Hungary.
5.3.66

At this tragic moment for our brothers and sisters in Ghana and Africa, we, as true patriots of Africa and our progressive friends of the world, feel it is our duty to express our moral support to you as a legitimate President of the Republic of Ghana in your struggle to bring back Ghana to its state of law and order.

We emphatically condemn the behaviour of the stooge, traitor and enemy of Africa, Ankrah and his masters. Imperialist America has proved to everybody, even to a fool, that she is not willing to live in peace with anybody due to her interference in Ghana's internal affairs during your absence on an important peace mission about Vietnam problem. It is a great lesson to all African leaders that the imperialists are still vigilant and they are using all their powerful manoeuvres to dominate our continent.

Dear Kwame, whatever manoeuvres the imperialists and their running dogs may try to use in order to blackmail Ghanaian and African people they are all doomed to a total failure, for the people are aware of them. We are sure that the Ghanaian people love you and that they are behind you, and sooner or later they will resist and free themselves from the new

169

slavery imposed on them by the traitors. We ask you kindly to offer your heart to those who dearly admire, honour and love you for what you have done for them. To any black man whose grandparents, brothers and sisters for years immemorial have been and still are under oppression, torture and exploitation of the imperialists, your name is a great name and you are for them and they are for you.

We admire and honour you for what you stood for and what you have been struggling for: the total liberation of the whole of Africa and African unity. These are noble ideals which have made you a great son of Africa. They will live for ever from generation to generation of Africa.

We send you our heartily felt congratulation for your new appointment as the head of both Republics of Ghana and Guinea. Our hearts and love are with you for the struggle ahead.

Long live Africa.

Yours in the struggle against the imperialists.

Bathurst, Gambia.
6.3.66

I, the undersigned, have heard with a great shock the irresponsible army rebellion against your esteemed person and government on the 24th February 1966. I wish to reaffirm, through the medium of this letter, my fervent support for your government, party, and your stand for the unification of compact but turbulent Africa. Your indomitability and intransigence in leading your people to a glorious independence will always go down in the annals of history of our continent as an inspiration to her sons and daughters.

Undoubtedly, Sir, you have served as an inspiration in our struggle against foreign supremacy, and you have served as an inspiration for political evolution in West Africa in particular and the continent in general. Your endeavour to unify dear Africa and to revive her culture and heritage are laudable. Africa is no longer prepared to suffer the irreparable loss of such great sons of hers, such as Ahmed Ben Bella and your honoured self through irresponsible rebellions such as those engineered by Major Ankrah and General Boumedienne who do not have the interest of their peoples at heart but are rather self-seekers instead.

Meantime, I am sure that the widespread indignation which is rising as a result of this will help to mobilise our forces to crush such illegally constituted governments as those headed by Boumedienne and Ankrah respectively. Your people who, through intimidation and wanton terrorism, could not celebrate jubilantly the 9th Anniversary of the glorious Independence of Ghana, will rise some day under your brilliant leadership and crush the illegal Ankrah regime. The terror and degradation this regime has brought to the people of Ghana and Africa are clear indications of its illegality.

Needless to say, you are assured of my indefatigable support and remember you are not alone in your struggle; the whole continent is behind you. I wish you long and prosperous life and I pray that providence will allow us all to see the day when the Ankrah regime shall climb down and be humiliated by the whole continent.

Long live Osagyefo.
Long live the dynamic C.P.P.
Long live President Sékou Touré.
Long live the O.A.U.
Long live African freedom and independence.

African student, Cambridge, England.
6.3.66

When I heard the news of the Ghana mutiny I felt so disappointed. Never in my whole life have I ever been so disappointed and felt so ashamed to be an African. I could not believe that I was listening to the B.B.C. and afterwards I thought "oh well, those imperialists could say anything, since you were in Peking trying to bring peace on earth and understanding among men." The imperialists manufactured stories to ridicule you and the work you intended to do for mankind. After I saw a T.V. transmission I said to myself—"Yes, the giant has fallen," and the imperialists knew that they could effect this iniquitous act only while you were out of the Republic and thought to work against you from behind. The imperialist world has never forgiven you and will never forgive you for the work you have done for the entire African continent. From the day Ghana became independent you told the crowd who were celebrating the independence of the new

171

Ghana that the independence of Ghana was meaningless unless it was linked up with the liberation of the whole of Africa. Indeed you followed that by calling several Freedom Fighter meetings in Accra and Accra became known by the imperialists as a den of iniquity.

Those of us who have been to Ghana to attend the Freedom Fighters' meetings will understand the cause of the imperialists' joy at your so-called downfall. Furthermore the speech that you made at the U.N. last time that you were there as the President of Ghana hit headlines all over the world that you were anti-West so-called civilisation. The speech you made at Addis Ababa at the first meeting of the O.A.U. in which you made an appeal to Africans to unite for survival made the whole imperialist world cry with a loud voice that you clearly indicated that you wanted to be the leader of the whole of Africa. Fortunately I was there myself and you mentioned nothing of that thought that you wanted to lead Africa. As a matter of fact you even then said that we should have a Bank of Africa somewhere in the Congo. Most of the English-speaking African countries are states which are independent today, I am proud to say they owe their independence to you Kwame Nkrumah personally.

I am one of the millions of Africans who would give his life to do anything to say to you, Kwame Nkrumah—I love you. May Providence guide you in all your future undertakings.

Cairo, Egypt.
(Translation)

6.3.66

President Kwame Nkrumah,
Leader of African States.
Greetings.

Last week, and since the latest events in Africa, especially the dishonest "coup d'état" made by the colonialist bandits in Ghana the free African country, I have been angry and unable to sleep. But today, I am calm and overjoyed to hear on U.A.R. radio of your safe arrival in Guinea, also of your presidentship of Guinea. The announcement of President Sékou Touré will enable you to lead the African liberation movement.

I recall the Arab Moslem leaders, like lions in battle, who

172

instantly gave up their leadership when ordered to do so, but never lost their enthusiasm.

I congratulate you on the confidence expressed in you by President Sékou Touré, who believes in African liberation. I congratulate you on behalf of the youth of the U.A.R.

We are with all our sentiments and hearts with you to the end. As for me, I am ready to fight anywhere to save the cause of freedom and peace in our continent of Africa. I would be greatly honoured to serve under your command against the colonialists and their puppets who seek only their personal profit.

For your information, I was a soldier in the U.A.R. Para-troops and fought against imperialism in our brother-land "Yemen."

I offer my deep thanks to President Sékou Touré, and offer my life for freedom and peace. This is a lesson we learned from our first teacher and wise leader President Gamal Abdel Nasser, who leads us from the military struggle to the battle to construct our land. He has transformed us to become good men in every sector of life.

We'll be victorious.

Bathurst, Gambia.

7.3.66

I pledge my firm support and implicit trust in you as the foremost African revolutionary and as the redeemer of Africa from the devastations of imperialism, colonialism and neo-colonialism. You have by exemplary hard work and enormous hardships built up Ghana to a high state of development, an example indeed to all states in Africa.

The Ghanaian people cannot and will never stand long a reactionary government constituted by a collection of brigands. The days of this wretched bunch of boot-lickers of imperialism are numbered. The Ghanaian people will rise and nip in the bud the marionettes of Western imperialism busy trying to arrest the revolutionary progress of Ghana and Africa. You have firmly established the Ghanaian people in the vanguard of the African Revolution. They cannot, therefore, tolerate the position of spectators when their brothers and sisters are but-chered by Western imperialist mercenaries. The cowards and puppets of Western imperialism will soon be brought to book for their treachery and wanton brutality. This small counter-revolutionary bunch of corrupt and myopic soldiers and policemen are not only betraying Ghana but are cogs in the wheel of progress.

All African revolutionaries fully understand what is going on. So long as the Continental Union Government of all Africa, that must be, is not here, imperialism will always be able to finance treason and naked exploitation.

Osagyefo, you are the voice and image of *all Africa*, as well as the voice and image of Ghana.

> Long live the heroic and revolutionary Ghanaian people.
>
> Long live Osagyefo Dr. Kwame Nkrumah, President of the Republic of Ghana.
>
> Long live scientific socialism.
>
> Long live all freedom fighters.
>
> Long live a Continental Union Government of all Africa.
>
> Long live the African Revolution.
>
> Long live African unity.

Lusaka, Zambia.

9.3.66

You receive this letter from a person you do not know, nor expect to know neither. But the fundamental reason for writing to you is this: that the Ghana problem is of growing concern in the hearts of Africanists.

There may be many who feel happy about what is happening in Africa today. These, if they exist, are the unfortunate few who have been swept into the political arena.

Whatever may be said about and against you, your very presence on Africa's political screen means a lot. Should you go for ever, true to say, Africa will be the most doomed continent on our planet. Already the vacuum is being felt, and no one can doubt it.

While you still live, God has chosen you together with many other true African leaders to build Africa for the generation after you, a perfect independent continent, unlike Latin America. I pray that for the sake of Africa you will solve the Ghana problem.

Should the Ghana problem not be solved, no African state

174

will ever feel safe. I fear that forces like those which exerted pressure in your armed forces may work to cause trouble in the place where you now lay your head. You and President Sékou Touré are true and sincere leaders of the Africa we wish to see.

In God's name do not let Africa and the coming generations down. Your history and the record of your activities will be incomplete if you do not solve that problem.

Kwame, fulfil your long and old-standing plans to build the Africa of your dreams.

I pray and hope that you will regard my little note as both a consoling and encouragement-giving letter.

Freetown, Sierra Leone.

10.3.66

I heard the news which I still cannot believe as being true concerning the rebellion against your lawfully constituted government of Ghana by some members of your police and armed forces. This is the greatest tragedy which if left unchecked will bring Africa with all its political and economic achievements a hundred years back. I pray to God that I may not live to see this day. I am hereby pledging my entire and resolute moral support to whatever course of action you intend to take in order to correct this treasonable act.

I have tried to follow the events in Ghana very closely, and have come to the conclusion that the rebellion was masterminded by the Colonial Imperialists with the backing of a few imperialist stooges in Ghana. Their stupidity and wanton acts will be corrected in due course. I am of the conviction that without your presence in the front line the battle against imperialism and neo-colonialism will be lost, and Africa will once more be infiltrated by foreign elements who will further their work of exploitation. The trouble in Ghana is mainly due to the fact that some imperialist stooges who want to amass wealth for themselves find themselves cornered by your socialist policies. Just as you said in your Independence anniversary broadcast from Radio Guinea, that the "development in Ghana under your regime is an open book"; this is quite true. I have not however visited Ghana but by looking at pictures and listening to radio broadcasts from imperialist countries, who now turn to say different things about your

175

regime I am convinced that Ghana had undergone a great change and is now fully developed. Many criticisms had been made against you after the rebellion concerning your economic development programme. The only reason for these criticisms is that the neo-colonialists still want to control the economy of Africa.

Judging from the words of your opening speech at the O.A.U. Conference in Accra last November: "History is made only by bold ventures and not by retreating in the face of difficulties." I know that you are not discouraged and will continue to fight to free Africa from colonial imperialist and neo-colonialist domination. You are the light of Africa, if you go off, the whole of Africa will lose its right path. Seeing all that is happening in Africa due to the work of imperialism, it is necessary to ask, who does not want to support a Union Government of Africa? Our brothers in South Africa and Southern Rhodesia have to be freed from white slavery, and the remaining colonial territories made masters of their own destiny. All this work has to be directed by right-thinking Africans like you. I cannot afford to miss you in the front line battle.

May I take this opportunity to extend my sincere and best greetings to one of Africa's greatest sons, President Sékou Touré. Never before have I the slightest belief that an African leader will be prepared to surrender his sovereignty for the sake of another leader. He has written a chapter in the great book of African history. We will always remember him as one who proved the reality of a Union government of Africa.

I have enough confidence that with the help of friendly countries and the resolute determination of the people of Ghana who are now being suppressed by a few military stooges you will soon make a triumphal entry to Ghana.

I wish you success in your struggle to liberate we, the people of Africa.

Long live African solidarity and a Union Government of Africa that must be.

Ghanaian student, Manchester, England.
12.3.66

I was surprised and indeed very sorry to learn of the unjust act by Ankrah in Ghana.

This news so annoyed me, that I felt, to express my feelings, I must write to you. I have always been a loyal supporter of yours, and proud to say I will remain so.

Indeed, Ankrah's illegal regime must be brought to an end.

I just thought I would write and add that if at any time you need volunteers to defeat Ankrah, I will be only too willing to stand by you.

I would like to add, that I am a fellow Ghanaian.

If you ever need support, please do not hesitate to write.

Your most loyal and obedient servant.

Ghanaian student, Leipzig, E. Germany.
13.3.66

No, those of us you were training haven't changed yet. We have now become more convinced than ever. You have always been our mouthpiece, you still remain our mouthpiece. What has happened is a horror and a disgrace to our race, an insult to intelligence and a setback to mankind. We detest stooges, we deplore their moves. No, we the youth remain undaunted. The ever burning flame of liberty you have lit in Africa keeps on burning, every second of it reminding us of woe, danger and enslavement. We will bear it high, we are convinced. Its glare is beyond Africa, it goes to our brethren everywhere. No less than a thousand times have you tried to show us the dangers of our independence, what the enemy can and does do. In no phase of our contemporary history has the danger been so naked. This is a warning to all.

No, it does not discourage us. No, we are not derailed. It consolidates our mission to humanity. Yes, we are convinced that the battle of our fathers, your mission to free us and war against hunger, disease and ignorance continues. Commander, leader, your soldiers the youth are ready. We have a mission.

Osagyefo, I am now doing my finals in medicine in Berlin. A few days ago I telegraphed you from East Berlin confirming my support—a sincere one, through thick and thin, and even at gun-point. I am small but am convinced, master. Please master, use me to fight on your side. It will be the most glorious honour to put down everything, to come home and to fight on an African front in the cause of dignity.

Master, I am convinced. I swear on oath to spill all my blood in your name and our mission. Not all have deserted

177

and those who have are unfortunate in that they have gone astray. They too will be convinced to come back soon. We rejoice at your well-being. We hail you and President Sékou Touré and rejoice to know even at the Accra prisons where death and tyranny are rampant we still have people who are convinced. Comrade Bing is also a big fighter. Yes, in our struggle, we have never known defeat. Hardships stimulate us. Forward we go, victory awaits us. Our fearless, courageous and dynamic Party, the C.P.P. under your leadership fights restlessly. We know no tiredness. "Forward ever, Backward never." Yes, we are right in the middle, we can't look back, we can't slacken.

> Viva Africa.
> Viva Sékou Touré.
> Viva Osagyefo.

Our course remains unchanged. The dogs may bark but the caravan moves on.

Dakar, Senegal.
(Translation)

15.3.66

Your personality embodies all the revolutionary movements which have overflowed the frontiers of Ghana. In spite of attacks directed from afar and insults organised against you personally you remain in Africa the Father of the Revolution, and whatever anyone says you are the unique upholder of true African freedom in our time, for all other African leaders to follow.

In all sincerity you are the guiding light for sincere nationalists everywhere who are struggling for the liberation of the peoples of Africa. Long before Ghana's independence you knew what independence was and how to let the people see it. You also knew what had to be done to gain this precious freedom and, when obtained, what had to be done to secure it. You provided the example by enduring all kinds of suffering, as man must do for his beliefs. For the colonialists spared no effort to discourage you and your gallant country in this work on behalf of all Black Africa. With your clear-sightedness you recognised and denounced the intrigues and manoeuvres by which the colonialists sought to delay their departure using men of straw whom they could manipulate from outside. Your wish that the people of Ghana should struggle to obtain lasting independence only shows that you were not to be put off by a nominal freedom for your country. You knew that independence is meaningless without economic, military and cultural freedom also. You defined precisely for them the fundamental criteria of real independence. You tried to show them that independent states should be composed of true Africans or more usually of nationalists. Such is the first condition of independence.

But in spite of your knowledge that man is not infallible you often had to depend on men who professed themselves to be revolutionaries but were in fact only doing so in order better to serve the cause of their imperialist masters. There are always traitors to any cause, professional double agents and that accursed type of person who possesses neither moral scruples nor patriotism.

In your sincere love for Africa and her exploited peoples you have appeared too confident in face of opportunists and traitors who seemed to work with you but were really stirring up trouble in the shadows. And yet you advised your Party to distrust people who placed their personal interests above national interest. You said that sooner or later those people would slip into treachery. How right you were.

To achieve African unity is a titanic labour—if it is not impossible. Yet your faith tells you that nothing is impossible and your will encourages you to surmount the obstacles.

You have begun realistically with what is possible. Once the programme is explained and defined with the objects of the struggle it will be easy for you to show the African people that there must be co-ordination of action in the conduct of operations, an equitable distribution of tasks taking into account multiple considerations of a practical order. You have succeeded with difficulty in inculcating into leaders of African states the urgency of unity and of Continental government. Alas I must stop at this point, vocabulary doesn't permit me to give you fuller details of what I feel and what I see in you, my dear and well-loved President, Defender of Africa.

I am entirely at your disposal hour by hour and day by day for the cause which is dear to us, and I wait impatiently to hear from you.

179

I. S. Isah, Leninsky Prospect 113, Friendship University, Moscow B—198, Room 407, U.S.S.R.
15.3.66

Kindly accept my unflinching support and loyalty to you. In fact I am shocked by the recent incident in Ghana. There is no doubt that this is the work of Imperialism. The people who took part in this rebellion under the name of the so-called National Liberation Council are die-hard enemies of socialism, criminals, power-drunken tribalists and enemies of the progress of the African peoples. There is no doubt that their days are numbered. History and time would prove them guilty of this criminal act. By this act, they have not only disgraced the Ghanaian people but also belittled the African Revolution which you started. You have distinguished yourself as an outstanding statesman, not only of Ghana and Africa, but of the whole world in general. The world will remember you in history as the father of the Ghanaian people and the foremost champion of African freedom, unity and world peace.

At this moment, men and women, because of their political and ideological convictions are being massacred at home.

Those who think that they can suppress the masses not to follow their leader to the cherished goal are just deluding themselves. For, as you said in your recent book "Neo-Colonialism," and I beg to quote, "For when all is said and done, it is the so-called little man, the bent-backed, malnourished, exploited, blood-covered fighter for independence who decides; and he invariably decides for freedom." Osagyefo, the whole of Ghana is behind you. We shall follow you to the last for in you we have found light, hope and guidance. Bullets alone cannot prevent us from following you.

Once again, I would like to express my loyalty and sincerity to you personally, the party and the government.

Ghanaian student, Belgrade, Yugoslavia.
15.3.66

This is the moment when the true sons of Ghana and Africa should sacrifice for the future of our dear continent. You fought a long battle in our Motherland, revolutionised the country economically, socially and culturally so that the poor will live in a good condition.

At a time when you were appealing for peace for the benefit

of mankind, raising the flag of Ghana and the whole of Africa, the moneyminded opportunists who refused to accept the glory of your perseverance and sacrifices have attempted to destroy the seed of your good work.

Uneasy lies the head that wears the crown is really an accepted fact. In your position with many plans ahead to build a state for the people and those yet unborn, I am strongly with my mite prepared to answer any call in which I am able to be considered to give, even making a sacrifice of my soul for the battle ahead. I am a Ghanaian student in this country.

Las Vegas, Nevada, U.S.A.

18.3.66

Sir, it saddens my heart to receive the news that my one great hero has been betrayed by a bunch of misled fools.

You sir, are surely the Redeemer. You are the only great man in all of Africa.

We here in America know as you must know, that the U.S.A. is the main enemy of Africa. Not only Africa, but all the dark races of the earth.

The reason I can say this is because you have spent some time in this country, and I'm sure you know what it's all about.

It's so sad that our people are so blind that they couldn't see what you were doing for them.

I'm one of the unfortunate ones. My great-great-grandfather was kidnapped from those very shores, 400 years ago. Sir, I'm fighting now as you must have fought for the independence of your country years ago.

I only wish it was possible to get out of this devil country and join ranks with you, and die for a just cause. We here don't have any way of fighting back. It's like the poor people living under Hitler in the thirties and early forties. Sir, there are hundreds of thousands of us here in this country that think as I do. We here don't stand a chance. Your great book on Neo-Colonialism is like a candlelight in a dark cellar.

All my friends that I know have purchased one, and I myself have purchased five for my library. We've all read your book.

I'm an ex-paratrooper, and once fought in the defence of

181

this country in Korea. I'm very highly trained in handling my enemy.

Now I would like to turn that skill on the ones who gave it to me. For as sure as I'm writing this letter I know that this country had a hand in what happened in Ghana. The C.I.A. is over there in strength undermining the free countries of the world.

Sir, I don't even know if you will get this letter, or if you'll answer it, as I know you are a busy man. But if you do find time to answer this letter it will mean so much to me and the people who worship your very name.

I have read that you will return to Ghana. Sir, I wish I had the honour of paving the way back for you, for all of Africa needs you. You are the one man who can save Africa if any-one can.

So may God be with you and all great men who have given so much for the freedom of his fellow men.

Chicago, Illinois, U.S.A.

21.3.66

Millions of us Black Americans were sick and hurt over your recent ouster from Ghana. We feel the Ghanaians have been badly misled and are blind to the international forces pulling the strings. Believe me sir, you have been badly maligned by the biassed press in this country, but we as negroes are assured of one thing

> "if white America was against you, you were the right man for Ghana."

Black America could tell your countrymen exactly how "white America thinks and acts"—to them you were the symbol of Black Power which she does not intend to tolerate in Africa or any place else. You were a man, Mr. Prime Minister, she couldn't handle—you refused to be a puppet, so consequentally you had to go—and so will every other leader in Africa—which as you well know is the purpose of the C.I.A. to overthrow any government which does not follow our line.

I hope some day to see you Prime Minister and President of Ghana again because Africa needs men like you—men who are for Africa, first and foremost.

Best wishes to you, Sir, and please be cautious.

Abidjan, Ivory Coast.
29.3.66

It is with tears that I address you this short message. I ought to have done so a long time ago but my delay was due to lack of a good channel through which my letter could safely reach you. In fact, I became senseless when I heard of your overthrow by the Ghana army and the police under your leadership. The neo-colonialists and the imperialists have overthrown Africa but not you, "Dr. Kwame"—so some of the African heads of state think.

Brother, permit me to join all honest and truthful creatures to share with you this critical situation in which we are unwillingly placed.

These imperialists, colonialists and neo-colonialists are hungry for they get not to eat as they did during their colonial rule. They have seen the key of the main gate through which they can pass to sup us, but I assure them they will not succeed on this neglected spot. Africans can be easily surrounded by our enemies if we let this so-called "N.L.C." take seed. What can such a minority party "N.L.C." liberate in this world if not prisoners? Oh ye faithful and honest members of the Convention People's Party. Forward ever for Victory is Ours.

Please extend my brotherly greetings to our brothers and leaders of Guinea and Mali for their efforts for the C.P.P. government and especially for African unity. Until I hear you speaking on Radio Ghana in due course I remain your brother.

African students, Moscow, U.S.S.R.
31.3.66

Circumstances embracing recent events necessarily prevented our earlier contact with you. As true apostles to your course and teachings, as real patriots of Ghana and Africa and staunch members of the DYNAMIC CONVENTION PEOPLE'S PARTY, it becomes imperative that careful assiduity be given to the grave neo-colonialist intrigues in Ghana before any statement could be communicated to you as regards our stand.

The nature of the battle which we are preparing to wage, calls for the reorganisation of our forces based on a qualitative transformation and the purging of all reactionary elements among us. In short the battle needs an organisation whose members are unreservedly dedicated to your person and the cause of Ghana. This, we have done, and now wish to acquaint you with the following points taken at a special representative meeting:

1. That the undersigned Executive members on behalf of the special members of the C.P.P. in the U.S.S.R. still recognise your person as the true and constitutional leader of Ghana and that we also still recognise the IMMORTALITY of the CONVENTION PEOPLE'S PARTY and you as the GENERAL SECRETARY.

2. That we are organising ourselves more strongly than ever before, so that we can be a force to reckon with in the battle against the neo-colonialist intrigues in Ghana and its puppet military set up.

3. That we are ever ready to respond to your clarion call to save our dear Ghana which is now on the neo-colonialist market ready to be sold to Britain, America and West Germany, we give you our oath of loyalty, support and service and we are prepared to fight to the last man for the realisation of this pledge.

We, however, wish to bring to your notice that we are sure of our practical and theoretical ability to organise ourselves but what we lack is the spiritual and moral weapon, and none ever can provide this except your person, through direct contact in the form of fatherly advice and guidance. We are now ready for a move but the green light is to come from you in a word of approval and direction.

We once again pledge our unflinching support to your personal leadership and stand in the cause of the African Revolution. Your support among the mass of African students studying here in the U.S.S.R. is unquestionable.

We wish to assure you that we believe we shall be victorious for history is on our side, and its wheels cannot be turned back, hence we await your word which will put life into the whole organisation.

       Forward Ever, Backward Never,
       There is victory for us.

Chicago, Illinois, U.S.A.
2.4.66

I am so mad and disgusted with black humanity that I can hardly look at myself in the mirror. Are we that blind and dumb that we can't see what the white man is up to? Must we pay for our silliness in blood, sweat and tears? When I heard all of the nasty things said about what you had tried to do for Africa and the world I sat down and did what I rarely do, cried. What of all the sacrifices, the headaches, the hard work and energy poured into making Ghana the kind of place anyone would be glad to call home; what of all the many things that have made the lives of the people a little easier after hundreds of years of colonial rule? People that had never lived in substantial housing, had never had running water, no electricity and other real conveniences and yet, there were those who dare say that under your regime nothing had been done and the people are worse off than under the yoke of the white master.

Don't think that I didn't understand when you kept repeating "unity." I could see many discouraging things during my stay in Ghana. Many people complained and most wanted all of the nice push-buttoned things and did not want to work for them. Many of them pestered the life out of me for a sponsorship to the U.S. I refused because I could see that you were going to have trouble out of these that are here going to school and otherwise. They are finished and of no service to Africa, because they want to be like Americans and that means trouble. If Africa or any part of Africa is to be saved, it will have to be done as the Soviets, China and Cuba have done. Close the border and don't allow anyone out or anyone in to contaminate them. The worst thing that could have happened to Africa, is the Peace Corps, founded for spying and brainwashing its subjects into followers of America. As I talk to young men from Nigeria who finished High School under Peace Corps teachers I think I am talking to American negroes.

I hope you are taking a much-needed rest and planning your next moves carefully. I believe in your ability and good judgment to finish the task of uniting Africa. I know that Ghana was just a stepping stone to your ambition to see a Free and United Africa. You said this over thirty years ago,

185

and I am not the least disturbed about your being barred from Ghana, because even I know, that until all Africa is free then none of Africa is free.

May God bless you and keep you secure from all harm, also your wife and children. And a pleasant bon jour to President Sékou Touré.

Freetown, Sierra Leone.

13.4.66

I am writing this letter from Sierra Leone to you, sympathising with your overthrow and at the same time congratulating you for your appointment in Guinea.

I am looking forward to when you will crush that rebellion in Ghana.

I hope that you are well and physically fit to be the leader of Africa some day. As you have said what has happened in Ghana is not a coup d'état. I agree with it wholeheartedly. If you are not in the Organisation of African Unity, the Organisation have gone 50 years backward, and it will not be achieved, and may God bless you in all your deliberations. May God give you a long life and a well body.

I am 16 years of age, pan-Africanist. Greetings to you and our brother, father lover of African unity, President Sékou Touré.

> Long live Osagyefo.
> Long live Sékou Touré.
> Long live O.A.U.
> Long live the Convention People's Party.

It's a pan-Africanist.

Ghanaian (no address).

17.4.66

I feel like addressing these few words to you before leaving this country. I hope I don't bore you.

I leave this country aware of the challenge that lies ahead of me at home. Don't be worried about my material support. My education will provide me with gainful employment at home. The welfare of those faithful followers who are here with you is our concern and responsibility. I wish there could be the possibility for me to send a few coppers out of my salary for their care-taking. Those of us at home don't need money for organisational purposes. Money has lured many true revolutionaries from achieving their objectives. All I need is that "God may grant me the serenity to accept the things I cannot change, courage to change the things I can, and wisdom to know the difference." My weapon is secrecy. It is only through secrecy that I can penetrate into every corner. I will succeed.

Dear Leader, I am tremendously inspired by your philosophical fortitude. You have correctly stated that there are two main reasons why you want to go to Ghana, namely the building of socialism and the success of the African Revolution. No other mission could be nobler. Your supporters are many. Rest assured that on your return home you have men, dedicated men, Africa's new men with which to reckon. Truly the old order changeth yielding place to new. The Ghanaian people have already begun to realise the need to lift their nation from neo-colonialist obscurity to commanding influence in domestic commerce and world trade. Just as lightning makes no sound until it strikes, our present revolution is generating quietly. When it strikes, the revealing flash of its power and the impact of its sincerity and fervour will display a force of frightening intensity. This is my challenge. Our people have already begun reciting their long list of grievances against the Notorious Liars Council. They have begun to recognise that they are now living on a lonely island of economic insecurity in the midst of a vast ocean of material prosperity. This is why I am fully optimistic. This is why I am confident.

My Leader, just as Socrates felt it was necessary to create a tension in the mind so that individuals could rise from the bondage of myths and lies to the unfettered realm of creative analysis and objective appraisal, so must those of us who stand by you see the need to create the kind of tension in the Ghanaian society that will help men rise from the dark depths of prejudice to the majestic heights of understanding. If we succeed in this endeavour, we have played a noble historic role. There certainly comes a time when the cup of endurance runs over, and men are no longer willing to be plunged into the abyss of despair. That is why our people will soon rise in unison against those rebels. That is why I am confident.

My Leader, I know that human progress never rolls in on wheels of inevitability. It rather comes through the tireless efforts of men who are willing to make use of the time.

Without this hard work, time itself becomes an ally of social stagnation. I am going to use this time creatively in the knowledge that the time is ripe to do the right.

Farewell, my Leader. It will not be long when we shall meet again with smiles.

Forward ever,
Backward never.

Nigerian student, W. Germany.
21.4.66

It is very sad news for us in Germany to learn of the regrettable incident which took place in Ghana in your absence. I hope by now all our telegrams sent to you c/o your Embassy in Bonn have been posted to you.

When I first got information of the plan in 1965 I wrote a letter to your secretary in Ghana and after some months I received a letter dated 28.9.65 signed by Mr. G. E. K. Doe the Ambassador inviting me to see him, so I went and gave him all the information I had but I doubt very much if this information reached your office for necessary action.

I do not need to mention the daily embarrassment caused to we Africans here by the German news and American radio telling the world lies about your administration. Please sir, so many African students are behind you, mostly we Nigerians, so in case you need us for anything we are ready to give up our studies and sacrifice our lives so as to support you.

We are convinced that without you Africa can never progress or free itself from colonialism both black and white. I am the organising secretary of both Nigerian and African students union here and we have been discussing things together. I hope that this letter will reach you. We are ready to answer your call any time.

Freetown, Sierra Leone.
23.4.66

I have previously written to President Sékou Touré in your favour. I wrote collectively with the other executive members

188

of the Pan-Africanist Youth Movement of Fourah Bay College and also singly as an individual, devoted to the aims and ideals of your socialist doctrines. Listening with meticulous attention to all your broadcasts, I was particularly delighted by your interview with Mr. Douglas Rogers over Radio Guinea just after your short but loaded speech on Sunday, 17th April.

My letters must by now make clear that I am an Nkrumaist. Particularly optimistic about your restoration to constitutional leadership, I have been gravely appalled to see your anti-imperialist cannons turned full swing against you. "Africa Today" broadcast daily over Radio Ghana at 3 a.m. was one of my favourite programmes. Such very factual and educative programmes now talk about the "corruption of Nkrumah" . . . . What was this corruption? It must be very mean of thinking people to obscure and distort facts, just because their imperialist masters tell them to begin a campaign of blackmailing, in order to destroy your work. Such imperialist propaganda can never make sense to people like me. The C.P.P. funds have become Nkrumah's personal property— what absolute nonsense . . . . Radio Ghana in "Africa Today" some time ago said that your positive neutralism in foreign policy was "too pro-East." This is maliciously false. It added moreover that in the drive towards your main dream, that of African Political Union, you had ignored the interests of other states and merely sought to get all other leaders to succumb to your will. The report elucidated this by the train-ing camps you kept in Ghana. But did you plot against any other sovereign states? NO. Instead, the people were being trained from African countries still suffering under colonial misrule. What actually drove you to give asylum to these political refugees was the interest you have at heart for Africa.

I am now prone to believe that even the newspaper "West Africa" is an imperialist organ. All they wish to see is African fighting African, perpetual bloodshed, socio-political insta-bility, and then fresh opportunities for re-colonisation. The paper has in fact been speculating coups in the most unlikely quarters. The accounts are given by expatriate superficial observers in the main cities, who have no contact with the feelings of the broad masses. Their accounts suggest that the Ghanaian rebellion is very popular. . . . . The people still keep resisting the army officers, but no imperialist newspapers

189

or radio station will ever broadcast these. They will never talk of the 6,000 people now detained. But they will publish beautiful pictures of Nkrumah's statue being torn down.

To me personally, Ghana in the history of Africa for the past two decades, has always represented a great water-driven mill which generates light to direct colonial Africa. We came to one obstacle and overcame it. Ghana was close to coming into combat with the second obstacle, when imperialists fearing the dynamism the rest of Africa would automatically be heated with, spurred on the band of brigands to rebel. They have diverted the course of the water which has been driving the mill. But the mill remains there. Soon, I hope, the water will take its former course, and the light will begin to shine again, and the second obstacle will be overcome.

What little analysis I have given you will only serve to illustrate the critical minds some of us have in supporting you. Never mind the blatant lies to discredit you and your work. Devoted friends always have critical minds, and will never be indoctrinated by childish imperialist propaganda in an era when the African can think for himself. Your ideals must be the ideals for the whole of Africa.

To comrade Sékou Touré, I will remain a true friend. I have come to realise his worth and what he means. To both of you I wish all the success you aim at in this great battle against neo-colonialism.

Devoted friend I ever remain.

Freetown, Sierra Leone.

23.4.66

I have the honour to write you this letter and I hope it will meet you in good health.

As a true African and a nationalist, I have been keenly listening to your inspiring broadcasts over the voice of the African Revolution, Radio Guinea to Ghana and Africa as a whole. And all the while I am more and more convinced that those sycophants and slaves of imperialism, who deceive themselves that they have overthrown the legal government of Ghana, are merely wasting their time and effort. Their days are numbered and the day of reckoning shall definitely come soon.

Mr. President, I assure you that on behalf of myself and

all the revolutionaries and true nationalists here, we only await your command. We are ready—always on the alert to come over right now. We shall lead any movement inside and outside Ghana as well to crush this shameful act of rebellion against the people of Ghana. We are at your disposal, ready to act.

The imperialists may think that they have a victory to gloat over. They are wrong. The flaming torch of African nationalism and the surging force of African political and economic independence shall forever glow and burn. Africa shall never rest, so long as the neo-colonialist does not abandon his erroneous self-strangling policies of blackmail and economic suppression. All over the world they are condemned. And they know that they are victims of their own folly. The revolutionary forces in their own countries shall eventually awake and crush them into oblivion. Even the aborigines of that tiny island nation, which still lives on past glories and political deception are now realising their position in the world today. They know that they have nowhere to stand and sooner or later, progressive forces in their midst will rise up to steer the country to its proper place. Though small in number, the progressive forces among them are well determined. And they shall triumph. We have seen many examples: People's China, North Korea, Vietnam, Cuba, Ghana, Guinea, Mali, U.A.R., Congo Brazzaville, Algeria, Sierra Leone, and Zambia and may others. All these are living examples of where the imperialists and neo-colonialists have frenziedly and desperately clung to their efforts to undermine progress and stability but they have consistently met with defeat after defeat; strategic, political and moral defeat. Many more are already on the way.

Osagyefo, do not be worried. Be at rest and you will see what Mother Africa has for you. Just as you have said, Africa is not dismayed. Ghana shall be free again. You have tackled many problems far more complicated than this—than bringing a few idiots to justice. The people of Ghana are not asleep. They are no children to be fooled. They only abide their time. But they shall act. And we shall join them at once. Victory is ours. Forward ever.

Mr. President, once again I assure you that we are ready. We await your orders now. We may even be forced to come over before your orders, because we can no longer wait to see ignorant fools meddling with the affairs of Ghana. We shall act.

My greetings to our great comrade and father Ahmed Sékou Touré. Greetings also to our mothers Fathia and Madam Touré.

Long live the African Revolution.
Long live the C.P.P.
Long live the P.D.G.

Lusaka, Zambia.

11.5.66

I meant to write to you after the army mutiny in Ghana. But I could not do this because I was at that time living in U.D.I. Rhodesia. I left that unfortunate country after being detained for 30 days and then served with a Restriction Order.

Anyway, I am glad to jot these few lines to you. I want to say how much we appreciate the great service you have rendered to mother Africa. I want to assure you that millions of Africans in Southern Africa are with you and wish you every luck in whatever you are planning. Your service to Africa shall never be forgotten. We trust that your powerful and patriotic ideas and ideals will triumph soon as the peoples of Africa begin to see the difference between chaff and good wheat. We mourn the passing away of the glorious Ghana which God enabled you to build. Indeed it is difficult to think of it as being still Ghana. We prefer to call it the Gold Coast. For this is no longer Ghana which was born in March 1957. But we are confident that Ghana and the whole of Africa will triumph against the enemies of her nationhood and greatness.

Under the separate cover, I am sending you a booklet by myself called "African Religion Rediscovered." I omitted four chapters from this book because the settlers who govern the country where it was published would not allow other chapters to be published. I trust that you will enjoy it. I would appreciate an acknowledgement so that I can be sure that you have received it.

My home is in South Africa. I am an admirer of Mr. Mangaliso Sobukwe's Party, the militant Pan-Africanist Congress.

May God bless you richly together with Mrs. Nkrumah and the children. Your work cannot be undone. What has happened in Ghana can only be a temporary set-back. Greetings to President Touré. We appreciate all he has done for you. We salute him for his brave stand for our fatherland—Africa, which the neo-colonialists want to rape again.

Bathurst, Gambia.

12.5.66

This is to inform you of my very deep concern and misgivings over the despicable and treacherous act of criminal rebellion which led to the regrettable overthrow of your government. Those army and police adventurers who are guilty of this act have betrayed not only Ghana, but the rest of progressive anti-imperialist Africa as a whole, and I am sure the consequences to them, and to all the imperialist and neo-colonialist forces who are behind it all, will be grave and calamitous.

No act of treachery, sir, and no amount of imperialist and neo-colonialist propaganda, whatever the scale, and however hostile, can destroy even for a moment, the nobility and permanency of your achievements for Ghana and for Africa. Nor, Mr. President, can they in any way affect your universally recognised standing as one of the greatest political leaders of this century, and possibly of all time—the honoured pace setter of the African Revolution. If the rest of Africa, sir, had heeded your advocacy for a Continental Union Government and for a Unified Military Command, these senseless military coups would never have happened. But let us hope that recent acts of vandalism in Ghana and elsewhere on the continent will accelerate the pace to a clear enough appreciation of the imperative necessity for a Union Government, not only as a bulwark against imperialism and neo-colonialism but as the only effective means of organising and bringing to fruition the economic, political and social regeneration of Mother Africa.

The army and police, by their own treacherous action, will destroy themselves. The intrepid Ghanaian masses cannot, under any circumstances, however fraught with trials and tribulations, tolerate the nakedness and brutality of a military regime, and sooner than most people believe possible will expedite your eventual restoration to power and to the centre of the African Revolution.

193

While wishing the Ghanaian masses Godspeed in their crusade of ridding the country, once and forever, of this treacherous and irresponsible clique of army and police adventurers, I wish to take the opportunity of conveying through your very dignified person, my unbounded admiration for President Sékou Touré of Guinea, and for the selfless and extremely courageous way in which he is contributing his very important quota towards the ultimate triumph of the African Revolution.

Long live the great Osagyefo, long live President Touré of Guinea, long live the African Revolution for a Continental Union Government.

Koidu Town, Sierra Leone.

15.5.66

Let me first of all say that all patriotic sons and daughters of Africa are with you in your struggle for African liberation. You will triumph. I have the firm assurance that in due course you will go back to Ghana and resume your post as the legitimate leader of that sad country. By the grace of God the Almighty and the help of father Sékou Touré and other patriotic African leaders you will go to Ghana again and overthrow the present rebel military government and take over, and also thrash the traitors there.

You need not worry, sir, I know the patriotic Ghanaians are always with you although they cannot admit that fact in the presence of guns and bayonets, but I am sure in due course those guns and bayonets will be nowhere. They will be just as if they are in cold water, and that will be your right time to take over.

I am sure the Ghana coup is the work of imperialists who are anxious to drink the sweet waters of Africa (to take our wealth from us). Woe on them, that will not be, you and Sékou Touré and others are quite aware of that. They will not succeed despite the help of their skilled African scholars. Africa will continue her incessant march towards the goal of FREEDOM.

Ghanaian student, California 95430, U.S.A.

23.5.66

I have already committed myself to our revolution, to

194

Ghana, Africa and to you, and in no way do I feel ready to compromise. I have served our Party (C.P.P.) and our country, Ghana, and Africa and intend to continue.

I am ready to come to Guinea to join you under any capacity, be it radio announcer or servant. The Pan-African students in the Americas organised a big rally in New York City and many Afro-Americans participated. I intend to send some of the distributed pamphlets to you.

Most Ghanaian students have had their scholarships withdrawn for mere suspicion of supporting you. Many senior civil servants have been imprisoned. By this unfortunate situation in Ghana, the African struggle has been put back 2,000 years.

But I assure you no human force can defeat the philosophy of Nkrumaism. For now, I don't know what my next step will be. I doubt very much if the U.S. government will renew my visa. Already the President of the Pan-African students has been deported together with the General Secretary and are now in Cairo.

It seems that there is no place of safety for African revolutionaries except probably Guinea, Mali, Egypt, or Tanzania. I am now recruiting graduating African students to work for their first year or two for Committee of Nine by working as distributors of cloth and food to the Freedom Fighters from African countries like Angola, South Africa, and many others. I am committed to the Pan-African struggle. It is an obligation not a mere rational preference. I have had since my last letter a rebuttal that Kofi Baako or Amoaka-Attah are dead. But I know that General Barwah has been killed. I have also recently received letters from very close friends and heard of the dismay of many of our countrymen. Many people who at the beginning supported the so-called revolt are now unhappy because tribalism is the order of the day. One can only get a good appointment if he is a Ga or Ewe.

I am planning to organise a newspaper dedicated to African Revolution. This may be produced here or in London.

Your advice is highly needed. We shall call the paper "The Nkrumaist." This will be publishing the goings-on in Ghana and other places. We shall be mailing it to many people in Ghana and right here in many places. Do accept my support once more in your person and office.

Long live the African Revolution.

African student, Minneapolis, U.S.A.
24.5.66

. . . . Those Ghana students here who love you have been
coming to meet in my apartment almost twice a week to
cogitate about the problem of Ghana, and sometimes I get
so much involved in thinking about the problem that I end
up in wasting all time for my studies, and many a time I cannot eat and just go to bed. . . . . Then finally I said to myself,
I have wasted enough time already, and most likely I will
flunk my economics and humanities test which I am supposed
to take tomorrow, why shouldn't I go on and write him? So
I sat behind the typewriter to write to you direct from my
mind be it in good English or bad . . . . provided that you
know that someone cares. I say someone cares, and it's me,
Sowa Dua, a Ga boy who came here on his own to do industrial electronics. . . . .

There are many Ghanaian boys here who love you, and
understand what you are doing. On the other hand, there are
some few indeed who are plain stupid and just hate you and
your government, they are those that cannot think and see.
I follow your line so closely that I will never despair, and if
you die I will do the same. Sometimes I know that as a human
being you will regret or be exhausted, but I say that all are
behind you except the fools.

Syed Riaz Ali, No. 4 Guru Teg Road, Krishan Nagar, Lahore,
Pakistan.

11.6.66

I have read that an international warrant of arrest has been
issued for you and in this connection I will advise you to have
full courage, patience, firmness and a good hope from God.

People come to me and take me to their houses for prayer,
and I have at all times found God favouring me.

So—I PRAY GOD FOR THE GOOD ACHIEVEMENT
OF YOUR PURPOSE.

Kumba, West Cameroon.
16.6.66

I write to appreciate your courageous leadership in the

196

liberation of all African people and of Ghana in particular. I lack words to express the role you play to stamp down the existence of colonialism, imperialism and racialism in Africa. Everyone in Ghana and abroad is well assured that the "National Liberation Council" has not been able to maintain the reputation and dignity of the Ghana nation since the February coup in Ghana.

I have nothing that I want to do other than join my friends in Ghana and elsewhere to pray for the downfall of the present regime and its stooges. I do honestly believe that the Almighty God will hear our prayers and remedy the unspeakable situation now in Ghana by bringing you back to Ghana.

I am sure that the Ghana February coup is a wrong imitation of some coup d'état in Africa—the one in Nigeria and in many other African countries.

I am a boy of about 23, a Cameroonian, with a primary education. I and many others are conscious of your importance in Africa. There is no doubt that you will soon take your position in Ghana.

Long live President Kwame Nkrumah.

Long live President Sékou Touré of Guinea.

Long live the citizens of Ghana who are loyal to President Nkrumah in spite of the torments they receive from the "N.L.C."

Mansakonko, Gambia.
22.6.66

I have the pleasure in getting the opportunity of extending my unstinted support for your struggle against the evils of our beloved continent. The general support which the Gambian youth and older generation have for you could only be hardly demonstrated through me. This is the case of Africa as a whole. When the imperialists engineer such renegades as Ankrah in their idiotic plans it surprises nobody in the continent. The fact that you are No. 1 son of Africa is shared by every African youth. The fact also that Ghana was No. 1 in achievements and respect cannot be disputed. Much is appreciated of you and by their propaganda of lies and stupidity we are not in the least MOVED.

Long live Nkrumah.
Long live pro-Nkrumahs.
Long live Ghana under Nkrumah.
Short live pro-imperialists.

It is a pity that although we tune in to you every Sunday and our club has bought a tape recorder specially for your speeches to be taped and heard everywhere in the Division, certain words cannot be quite interpreted to the Gambians. I shall appreciate if you send me all the series of speeches over Radio Guinea since your arrival there.

I and my club (Nkrumahist Young Revolutionaries) are at your disposal any day you appeal for us. WE ARE DETER-MINED.

Please extend our greetings and admiration to your comrade Ahmed Sékou Touré.

Senator Dudley J. Thompson, Q.C., 62 East Street, Kingston, Jamaica.

22.6.66

I was very glad to have even your short note of acknowledgement and more glad still to see that both your health and spirits are as high as ever.

Do keep me in touch. However small and however remote I may be I should like to contribute my share in gratitude for what you have done for all of us. This is only a small phase in our history starting from the days of George, Jomo and others. Incidentally do you still hear from Jomo? I am very pleased to see that Nyerere and his immediate followers still strongly support you.

Remember my offer still holds good and any time you wish to recuperate, there is a home, pleasant garden and *all* the facilities that a young man who needs to rest from his dreams and prepare to fulfil them can desire. Just cable me the word "I am ready to come" and everything within my power including your passage and stay will be at your disposal.

We are passing through a peculiar phase just now. As I write, some three hundred-odd policemen and army with helicopter and water police support are storming certain slum areas where the poor but faithful have been resisting the oppressions of a neo-colonial government. They will of course lose and men will go to jail. Fingers are being pointed directly at me but of this I have no fear. My own leaders have already suffered in this way. If it is to be it will be. One has no escape from duty. One is a coward and a fool who tries to escape from destiny. I believe the immediate farce will be over in a week or two but unless a new socialist approach to satisfy the hopes of many can be put into effect we shall be lulled by our own Calypso mentality into the uneasy atmosphere of the luxurious tourist affluence for the few and the docile complacency of the suffering many until such time . . . .

I hope you will find time to write me a letter, and please take my offer very seriously.

Mahalpye, Bechuanaland.
4.7.66

First and foremost let me extend my hearty greeting to you and all the people of Ghana with you. The imperialists have staged full force come-back in Africa and Asia. We are aware of this and it is for all revolutionary forces to heighten their vigilance to work side by side with you. We also hope that the puppet states in Africa who always said that Nkrumah is plotting to overthrow their government will recall what you have long advocated.

The question of Rhodesia is now at a standstill. African states now think this is Kaunda's baby. They are not worried about their four million brothers in Rhodesia. All conferences have come to a standstill. There is not even a word about a meeting of the O.A.U. All we see in the imperialist press is that Nkrumah was a dictator. Most of the people begin to see why you always advocated African unity, and an African High Command. When Ghana gained its independence you said that the independence of Ghana was meaningless unless it was linked up with the total liberation of the African continent. You advocated for the establishment of a Union Government with all states represented in the Upper House and the Lower House according to population. Ghana the home of all revolutionary freedom fighters is temporarily closed, and some reactionary African states have taken advantage of this to send back the freedom fighters who took refuge in their countries. It is a proof to the people of Africa that you were a stumbling block in their way. They are now showing us their true nature. My firm conviction is that the military regime in Ghana is a temporary setback in Ghana's revolution, and that under your leadership the Ghanaians will defeat the reactionaries backed by U.S. imperialist, British and West German militarists.

In conclusion, I wish to thank the revolutionary leaders of Africa who took a stand in this issue, President Nyerere, President Keita, and President Touré. I hope that with them you will lead the revolutionary struggle to the end.

Dr. Nkrumah we need you, Africa needs you, and the whole world needs your ideas. Today in the world all favourable conditions are with the revolutionaries and unfavourable for the imperialists.

My best regards to the people of Ghana and their beloved President.

Yours in the struggle for the total liberation of our motherland and the union of all African states.

Nigerian student, Isleworth, England.

6.7.66

Strange as it may sound that a young lad of my type should be writing to you, and more so that I am a citizen of Nigeria. I would have written to you earlier since that last unfortunate disturbances in Accra, Ghana, but sincerely I hadn't the courage until presently.

I am at present studying law in this country and since my full age of discretion I have always been one of your admirers, and I only wish that we had at least five good statesmen in Africa with the same principles as yours.

Never mind and just keep smiling as those rebellious elements will soon come to terms with their consciences. If not, they are definitely going to lead Ghana into wilderness.

However, it is historians who will show to the yet unborn Ghanaians that you saw your country in darkness and gave them light, that Ghana, as small as it is, was highly and gloriously magnified.

Lagos, Nigeria.

19.7.66

This so-called overthrow makes me laugh. Ankrah and his men are just gambling perhaps they may win (as they think). They are deceiving themselves. They are bound to fail. Anyway this is not the time to talk generally so I beg to go straight to the point.

I am a boy of 21 years of age. My father is a Yoruba and my mother is yours, a Wassaw from Nswam. In short, I am a Wassaw. I came here very recently and was a member of the Ghana Young Pioneers.

Osagyefo, I want to fight for you if only you can and will bear all the expenses of training me to be a guerrilla fighter. If you will also promise to keep me in the Ghana army (I do not ask for any post) after you have been brought back to power, or if you will compensate my people if I die in the fight. This is all I need from you and I shall fight for you to the last drop of my blood if you agree with me. Do not reject me, please, for nobody knows who can help. I am physically fit, very strong and obedient. I am an Nkrumaist. I remember sincerely promising to live by the ideals of Osagyefo Dr. Kwame Nkrumah, founder of the state of Ghana and initiator of the African Personality. I shall never break this golden promise. Please never mind any grammatical mistakes and any wrong words in this letter but please mind the "idea."

I promise before man and God to fight to the last for you, if only you can do what I have asked. Train me to use arms and wait and see if I am effeminate.

To hell with Ankrah. Nkrumah, Ghana is behind you. Long live Nkrumah and Sékou Touré. Long live Ghana, Guinea, Mali.

T. R. MacLachan, 49 Dalberg Road, London, England.
6.8.66

You may be surprised at this letter coming to you from England—and from a non-African at that.

The fact is, I have been reading the texts of the speeches you have been making to your people in Ghana from Radio Guinea over the past few months. These speeches as you probably know, have been printed in the journal "Africa and the World." Reading your speeches, your encouragement and call to action to the people of Ghana has reminded me of the war-time speeches made by the then Prime Minister of Britain, Winston Churchill. Of course, please do not think I am comparing you with Winston Churchill apart from the speeches, which in his case spurred the people of Britain on to victory over fascism and in your case are, I hope, spurring the people of Ghana to victory over fascism also. Apart from that, I would say that any similarity between yourself and Churchill is non-existent; he stood for privilege and reaction, for the old order of things. You stand for a better life for all people, the development of Ghana under your guidance has been proof of that.

You may well ask, why do I, a British person who has never been to Africa, write to you? Well, I have been very impressed by the way you have led Ghana from being a backward colonial country to the first country of independent Africa, the way you have built it up in the past—and will do so in the future as well. I fully agree with your idea of not only a free Africa but a united Africa also. At the moment, let us face it, Africa is in the grip of imperialism and neo-colonialism, but things will not always be that way; sooner or later the real Africa will emerge victorious and the imperialists and their agents will have to face the wrath of the people. Another reason for my support and admiration of you and what you have achieved in a few short years for Ghana is due to the British press. You may be rather surprised at that, especially if you are familiar with the British press, as you surely must be. I should explain that my late father was one of the old British socialists, back during the early years of the present century. One of the things he taught me was that if the capitalist press praises you, watch out, you were going wrong. Since Ghana became independent several years ago, I have never seen the name of President Nkrumah mentioned in such papers as the *Daily Express, Daily Mail, Daily Telegraph,* etc., without a torrent of criticism, sneers or plain abuse. Remembering my late father's counsel, I have thought "President Nkrumah can do nothing right, according to them. That means he must be doing what is right for Ghana and its people." Further study of the matter has proved that you have done right for the people of Ghana, and when the present pitiful mob are removed, will continue to guide your people to further successes and happiness.

Finally, I am not going to say that I hope you will return to Ghana, because I know that you will as surely as night follows day. May your return be very soon.

To yourself, to the people of Ghana, to the people of all

Africa, I wish a happy and peaceful future. Long live Africa and the great people of Africa.

R. B. Keenoy, 8 Aldbourne Road, London, W.12, England.
16.8.66

I want you to know that I fully support your struggle and the struggle of your party in Ghana and Africa and the world. I have read some of your books and am convinced that your ideas and policies are the right ones for Ghana. I see that it is of the greatest importance that the rule of law and the C.P.P. replaces the corrupt fumblings of the imperialist lackeys who are bringing despair and danger to the Ghanaian people.

However, I share the conviction of Geoffrey Bing that either you or consciencism will return to Ghana.

You must never give up the fight because the same battle as yours is being fought or is to be fought in Vietnam, in the Congo, in Zimbabwe, in Indonesia and in South Africa and South America and in many other parts of the world.

Ghanaian student, Kherson, U.S.S.R.
21.8.66

I am a Ghanaian student in the above school and I want to declare my unflinching support for you, now and forever. I want to join the progressive people in your service for the building of socialism in Ghana, Africa and the world over, and I am prepared at any time to give my life for it. I am ever ready to do anything which will lead to your triumphant return to Ghana as President.

I am almost 29 years old (born on 29th November 1937) and hail from Akim Akroso, a small village between Agona Swedru and Akim Oda and I am an old boy of Adisadel College where I obtained my West African School Certificate in 1957. I have finished my three years' course in marine navigation and piloting in the Soviet Union here last July and I am now a qualified maritime navigator; but the Soviet Government have kindly allowed me to do further nine months sailing in their ships to increase my practical knowledge.

I was not a member of your, and our, Convention People's Party before coming to the Soviet Union, and it is here that I understood the need for building socialism in Ghana and Africa, and now that I understand it I am prepared to do anything to help achieve it. I wrote to the Soviet Authorities through the Director of our marine school to be allowed to stay here until the overthrow of the present fascist-pro-imperialist government in Ghana; but whom do I expect to overthrow the government for me to enjoy fruits of it; I should join the progressive forces in Africa. I am six feet one inch tall, strong in body and sound in mind and I should use my strength and little knowledge for the suffering millions in Africa.

I am presently going to sea and I shall return in May 1967 and I hope and entreat you to tell me what to do by the time I return from sea—please dear Osagyefo, do it, tell me what to do else I shall get a broken heart. Please I am not doing this for my personal gains now or at any time. I just want to do something in my small way to help the millions of Africans who are living in poverty.

Buea, West Cameroon.

22.8.66

The recent underground conspiracy in Ghana by the Western traitors and their domestic useful tools.

I write to congratulate you for your strength of character in facing the Western traitors and their stooges for the present chaos and confusion created by them in your beloved Republic of Ghana.

In the first place we of the African revolution are aware of your positive exposure to the world relating to what took place in Ghana during your official visit to the Far East. We are in no doubt that the neo-colonialists played on the GRAB mentality of men in uniform, also the colonial orientated intellectuals and professionals gave good support to this unwarranted and destructive state of affairs as seen in Ghana today. This unthinking mob of jackals continue to gallivant and pride themselves on their ignorance and stupidity by making idiotic and meaningless statements over the radio, etc., without foundation. Such utter rubbish could only be accepted by simpletons and over-credulous people who do not know even the basic history of Ghana as late as 16 years ago.

Secondly, it's well known that the colonialists and imperialists were severely beaten by you in Ghana, and when the time is right it would be absolutely no problem to put their quislings and lackeys down on bended knees. The arrogant idiots temporarily turn light into darkness, but the forces of light shall return and prevail, this is evidently clear as the sun goeth down in the west. OSAGYEFO, you have the progressive forces of nature more than ever with you now, also the vigilant elements at home and abroad are with you in this time of trial, and in due course you shall triumphantly return to your dear Ghana, this is most certain, as nature is the true test of time. Operation CRUSADER shall surely get even with these scamps, traitors, and imbecile tools of their Western dregs of humanity .

As a PAN-AFRICANIST and a devoted admirer of the philosophy of PAN-AFRICANISM, I have implicit faith that when the time is right you shall definitely for the second time LEAD the militant masses in Ghana to final victory and to fulfil their hopes and aspirations. Long live the OSAGYEFO! Long live the dynamic forces of GHANA. Long live African Unity.

Yours in the struggle against the enemies of human progress.

Mohammed Sulaiman Jaffery, T/85 Railway Bungalow, Parbatipur, Dist. Dinajpur, East Pakistan.

11.9.66

On this happy occasion, the anniversary of your birthday, I have great pleasure in extending to you the expression of my most cordial sentiments and heartiest felicitations.

Your historic contributions as a gallant gentleman, a great African, an intrepid politician and statesman of unquestionable political skill and undoubted sincerity, and articulate exponent of lasting peace and freedom to the creation and construction of Ghana, to the unity, solidarity and harmonious understanding of millions of people in Afro-Asian world will live for ever in history and evoke the gratitude of succeeding generations. You are one of those men whom neither their country nor their friends and admirers can forget.

I wish and pray to Almighty God for your enduring life and perpetual happiness on your happy birthday, and hope that your long experience and wise counsel would remain available to Afro-Asian countries for many more years to come.

May you kindly accept this humble presentation of a Pakistani student's great affection, profound respect and abiding admiration for you.

Catherine Walton, Gairnshiel Lodge, Glen Cairn, Aberdeenshire, Scotland, U.K.

28.9.66

From the depth of an old heart I send a message of trust in, and affection for you.

I've read your books (not the last one). I've longed for Ghana to work her way to the pinnacle of what a modern state can and should be. I've noted your acts of outsize understanding (piercing, without humbug, to the centre of a problem): and of your curious gentleness, very precious in these days; and I've raged at the British press for wicked unfairness in reporting.

I've quarrelled with *The Guardian* about their infuriating avoidance of connecting facts that came to hand.

It is my joy to meet people who think for themselves a bit and see further and deeper. There are many. So I want to send this message. It is from an old woman who feels it laid on her to be guilty for her country's failure in human relationship.

Very best wishes.

Ghanaian student, Studentenheim, West Germany.

1.10.66

I have taken this opportunity to write to you today in order to let you know how sorry I feel for the ungrateful accusations by those traitors of Ghana and Africa, those tools of imperialism, colonialism and neo-colonialism of Africa in Ghana against you. Frankly speaking, I haven't been able to get a good sleep since those traitors betrayed us. Sometimes, I feel like weeping because our only hope of survival is you.

Since this disgraceful action was taken against you in Ghana, I have written many letters home deploring the activities of our traitors. I made my parents understand that they would never hear from me any more if ever they wrote a word of praise for those traitors in their letters. I said also that I would then eventually change my nationality. Most of my letters were seized by the so-called "N.L.C." Our Embassy in

Bonn was contacted and instructed to do everything possible to enable the withdrawal of my scholarship. Though my scholarship wasn't awarded by your legal government, the organisation responsible for my scholarship has withdrawn my stipend since June this year. Those traitors in Ghana think that by so doing, I would support them.

I know that it has been difficult for me to continue with my studies without a scholarship. All the same, I can't support traitors for the sake of a scholarship. I shall do everything possible to finish up without their support.

Yes, Mr. President, it may interest you to know the effect this disgraceful action has had on students here. I can assure you that those who even used to be against you when you were in power now support you. Your absence in these few months has shown them that there is no better ruler in Ghana apart from you. More students support you now than formerly. Others are afraid to voice out their sentiments openly for fear that their scholarships would be withdrawn. Every student here knows that you gave us everything that a nation needs—pride, prestige, respect and national consciousness.

The back to colonialism drive by those nationwreckers will never last long. I am sure that you are doing everything possible to save us and Ghana again. We will support every action taken by you, even if military, in order to seize our beloved country from those tools of imperialism, colonialism and neo-colonialism.

You should also not forget, Mr. President, that there are hundreds of students here who share the same ideas with you and who will always stand by you. Personally, I shall never be happy until I hear that you have regained power in Ghana. From that day on shall I sleep in peace.

I send you my warmest greetings and wish you a speedy action in order to save Ghana.

Ghanaian student, U.S.S.R.

20.10.66

I am a student, calling you today from the Union of Socialist Soviet Republics. I study in the Kiev State University at the International Relations faculty. I am on first course.

I came to the Soviet Union with a scholarship from Ghana Government of which you were then the head of state, and I hope you are the head and will be for ever.

Please, my ear was not deaf to what took place in Ghana on 24th February during your absence. However, there is still happiness and courage that without you Ghana will never be free, and will encounter perpetual difficulties. This will not affect Ghana alone but Africa as a whole.

According to history Africa has once come under the British colony for several years during which the natural resources of Africa were taken away to develop Britain and the people of Africa subjected to famine and hunger. The blood of our forefathers was betrayed in the hands of these colonial powers by means of slavery and at the long last named Africa a dark continent, but it seems some of the people in Africa are not yet up with these colonialists. Africa must be a man well armoured without depending upon one who just possesses a long proboscis for blood sucking.

Ghana is now in the hands of the imperialists. In fact, we the younger generation are pushed down into graveyard if you do not wake up and save us. SAVE US, SAVE US, OSAGYEFO, else we die. If we are able to save ourselves from the lions and unite ourselves we shall also be fearless as sea water.

According to Bible, Socialism was first practised by Christians and called themselves brothers and sisters, but Africa is the land of Christians and why do some of the people not understand socialism? Oh dear, stand up again, but for this we in the Eastern countries are fully sharing hands with you.

The so-called national liberation council of Ghana has reversed Ghana far to the past 20 years, and for so long after the coup has been commenting on cassava, milk, sugar, Beatle shoes and American shirts and nothing better for the people. What are all these for? If cassava, milk, sugar, Beatle shoes and shirts are the necessary commodities for the people and the development of the country then, why should the state farms be cancelled and the factories be given to foreign enterprises? This time, it is not the developing of the country and the people as a whole, but a development by tribes and families. The jobless is now the servant to the high ranked men, and the poor is the servant to the rich. Since we need a good defence for the people of the country, education for the people and not for the rich alone, provision for the good health of the people and not for the rich alone, and the good provisions for the coming generations, you are the one who can be our head.

Please, in order not to be discouraged, sir, try to reply to me. I wish you good luck.

Freetown, Sierra Leone.
1.11.66

I would have written long before this time, but as you know we live in a world of mistrust and suspicion and as such, one just has to be tactful about many things. When I heard the ungrateful news I was shocked to my bone marrow. At first, it sounded in my ears as a wild rumour that suddenly took credence because I was not the least expecting the soldiers to have been so rebellious and insane to you and the nation as to have induced to insidious propaganda by colonial indoctrinated stooges. My heart laments greatly for the destruction of some of your good works and also for myself, because our ruling party had previously recommended my admission into your ideological institute, an institute I had long planned to attend, because if the future Africa should stand on her own, after smashing completely the fetters of colonialism and neo-colonialism it is we the youth who must be ideologically trained for the maintenance of the African Personality.

My conception about the rebellion is that it is the result of those who want to bring back and perpetuate colonial rule in Ghana and as a last resort to exploit state by state in the whole continent of Africa. The now temporarily formed "National Liberation Council," as I view it, embodies treacherous, prodigal and capitalist elements who think that everything for the benefit and progress of man is a suppressive ideology. My advice, sir, is that you summon courage. The courage you summoned that brought you to free Ghana from the yoke of colonialism and imperialism when you achieved independence, and which I am doubtlessly sure shall take you back to Ghana this time to lash out against neo-colonialism.

N. K. Sanyang, 21A Dobson Street, Bathurst, Gambia.
23.12.66

I have to thank you from the bottom of my heart for your reply to the letter I had previously written you, expressing my profoundest shock and disappointment over the despicable

209

overthrow of your Government. That reply, together with the wonderful speeches you delivered over Radio Conakry to the valiant masses of Ghana, will ever be treasured by me as a memento of one of the most remarkable personalities of our century.

I am more than passionately convinced, sir, that whatever else the future may hold, the principles of the Ghanaian Revolution, which form the corner-stone of your political philosophy, will be the main determinant of the ultimate destiny of Mother Africa. Imperialism and neo-colonialism may continue to subvert the fundamental unity of the African continent and may use the meagrely-rewarded services of nationally-negative elements to frustrate any leader or scheme dedicated to advancing the welfare of our peoples. But this system, as abhorred in the sight of God as it is in men, will inevitably be overtaken by the disaster that it so rightly deserves.

Those who think that imperialism and neo-colonialism are mere clap-trap words used by those who are inveterate enemies of man are only living in a cloud-cuckoo land of self-deception. That the danger from this system is real can clearly be adduced by the surprising, almost frightening rapidity at which progressive African leaders are being systematically eliminated by coup d'états, engineered by imperialism but practically implemented by those of their nationals who can at best be described as traitorous and reactionary. It is monstrously absurd and at the same time grossly unfair to assert that these leaders, after successfully breaking the shackles of imperialism to lead their nationals to the rarified atmosphere of Olympian freedom and self-determination, have suddenly become so dictatorial as to deprive them of the very freedom for which they sacrificed so much. Never was a more stupid calumny uttered! On the contrary, reactionary leaders have been dubbed as progressive, democratic and sensible, even though they have never hesitated to sacrifice the vital interests of their countries on the altar of neo-colonialism, and have thereby forfeited the support and affection of their masses. They have been kept in power only by imperialist machinations and the flouting of fundamental principles of human rights.

It is inconceivable and morally abhorrent, sir, that a man who has unselfishly placed the interests of his country and his

210

continent before his own, should encounter treachery from the hands of the people whose cause he so valiantly championed! But so, Mr. President, were the prophets rejected. There are certain intrinsic qualities, however, transcending beyond the merely material or the merely physical which, whatever else reactionary and treacherous forces may do, human agencies can never destroy, and among these is the stamp of greatness. That you have been endowed with this quality in the highest degree, even your most implacable enemies admit, and they are legion.

Men will always remember, not without affection and gratitude, that it was your single-minded dedication and extraordinary qualities of leadership that made independence in Black Africa possible. This alone, Mr. President, without the other colossal achievements for which you are world-famous, is sufficient to earn for you a permanent niche in the gallery of the very great. Come what may, your name will continue to reverberate across the corridors of history.

Whatever the mysterious future holds for me, as a human being with finite capacity, I do not honestly know, but of this I am more than certain, that whenever I am called upon (and I am sure I will be) to play an effective part in the political life of my country and of Africa, I will always look upon your career and the principles for which you stand as the guiding light of my life.

Please convey my sincerest greetings to that stalwart nationalist, President Ahmed Sékou Touré of Guinea and members of his dynamic Government. And remember that I always look forward, with pleasurable anticipation, to your triumphal entry into Ghana. I am sure it will come sooner than our enemies expect.

> Long live Osagyefo the Great.
> Long live President Touré of Guinea.
> Long live the African Revolutionary Struggle.
> Down with the hydra-headed monster of imperialism.

Lecas Atondi, Professeur des C.E.G., B.P. 4085, Brazzaville.
1.1.67

It is a great honour for me, a mere poor Congolese, to write you, the very President of Ghana. Doctor, all revolutionary

Africans are with you, and they believe in the final victory of the heroic people of Ghana.

British and American imperialism think that they will be able to conquer Africa; strictly speaking, they can't, they are merely paper tigers. I am sure Africa will shake colonialist domination and its toads will be defeated.

Dear Doctor, Lumumba, Ben Bella and you are enlightened combatants, living examples of courage, freedom and independence. I remain faithful to your principles of freedom and revolutionary wisdom.

In Ghana and Algeria, hooligan soldiers are plotting against their own countries with British and French imperialism. They betray Africa. However, I am considering African Revolution will triumph. I am with you.

Dear Doctor, I have a son, I would be pleased if you granted me permission to give him your name; he would be called: ATONDI NKRUMAH. I inform you that everybody calls him by this name. I thank you sincerely, in advance, it will be an honour for my son and myself.

I would like to receive your news.

President, the Congo is with you, Ankrah and his henchmen shall be defeated, it is a law of history. Dear Doctor, a New Year begins and I wish you a Happy New Year. My little boy wishes you the same greetings.

Gambia.

12.1.67

In celebration of the feast of Ramadan, I take chance of wishing you many happy returns of the occasion and wishing you all the good you may wish for yourself and Africa. I wish from the very bottom of my heart that Allah, the almighty, guide and protect you from the evil intentions of all enemies and I further wish that Allah enables you to take control of Ghana very soon.

Please remain assured always that your great ideals will prevail as long as the world lasts and that your ideology of Nkrumaism will one day be accepted by Africa. That being so, continue your vital teachings and preachings to further awaken Africa and the world against the intrigues and machinations of imperialism, colonialism and neo-colonialism. You will surely triumph over your enemies and the enemies of the

African liberation movement. Forward ever, Backward never, you will once more defeat the treachery of imperialism.

I shall be most grateful if you will direct me as to where to get your books more especially the latest entitled, "Neo-colonialism: the last stage of imperialism." I am deeply interested and concerned in everything about you and because I am interested in politics, I shall follow your teachings and methods to the letter whenever I take up politics. Whenever you have chance, sir, write other books for the guidance of Africans and mankind at large for without doubt the imperialists and their agents have, I am sure, destroyed the precious and invaluable work you did in Ghana.

I should like to get the broadcast talks you made over Radio Guinea after the unfortunate incident of last February. Whatever the odds, please look forward to 1967 with great optimism that you will once more rule Ghana and actively continue the liberation struggle to free every inch of the African continent from imperialism, imperialist domination and exploitation. Never give up hope for the mass of true African nationalists are behind you and victory is sure to be yours for your cause is just. The imperialists and their agents will come to shame before too long.

Long live Nkrumaism, the ideology for Africa. Long live Presidents Nkrumah and Touré. Long live the African liberation struggle and African continental union government, which must be.

May God save you from all enemies (Amen).

Please take the finest care of yourself always.

Ghanaian student, London, S.W.19.

1.3.67

I will firstly introduce myself—I am a Ghanaian student in U.K. and a staunch member of the C.P.P. (under your leadership) despite the fact that the so-called "N.L.C." have banned it.

As one of your best admirers in London, I feel that I must write to greet you sincerely on the coming 10th Anniversary of Ghana's Independence.

Although you are not in Ghana at present which many people would prefer your presence for this celebration, but

213

I can only say that wherever you are, we are there in spirit with you for this Anniversary.

May I pray for the God guidance for your safe return and lead us again as a great Statesman of Africa and the world as a whole.

May success crown you in your efforts so that we can join you to celebrate the 11th Anniversary with you in Ghana.

With my best wishes.

Long live Osagyefo! Long live C.P.P.!

Ghanaian student, Hamburg, W. Germany
5.3.67

Perhaps you might be aware of the hardship to which, under the said military junta, your aspiring students here have been exposed. We can feel the tremendous difference of our care and well-being in your time and with this new government

Unprecedentally quite a good number of us have lost our awards for no just cause; an action which has been widely criticised and felt improper for a nation which you have built up. There is at present a deep-seated feeling amongst us who have lost our awards, with the strong sympathy too from those unaffected. Perhaps it's needless to describe to you the extreme hardship to which we have been subjected by this action.

After a lobby we have felt ripe enough to re-organise ourselves in support of your return home. Indeed the feeling and determination is not only for our awards but also looking back in dismay, for example, the mess and the disgust with which the last Commonwealth Conference was held; with the buying-off of our leaders on the Rhodesian issue—which was inconceivable with your presence and dynamic search for action. We all have you at heart, realising what a champion and bulwark we have miss. We need you, for your ideals and action have truly achieved for Africa within a decade what otherwise would not have been possible in a century.

Dear Osagyefo, please we need your help in every way possible. Our studies are in danger due to this hardship imposed.

May you live longer and do more for us.

In a high expectation to hear from you soon.

Mr. Harald Berntsen, 3218 Studentbyen Sogn, Oslo 8, Norway.

18.3:67

The Norwegian Students Association has for more than 150 years been the major forum for debate among Norwegian intellectuals, and more than any other independent society it has had a tremendous impact on Norwegian cultural and political life. Many prominent speakers have visited the Association during the last few years—Eisenhower, Macmillan, Mikoyan, President Nyerere—to mention a few.

The meetings which are held on Saturdays gather usually 700-800 students, graduates, professors and members of Parliament. The lectures are always covered by the press.

Traditionally candidates of different political views are competing for the presidency of the Association each semester. I am running with support from the socialists, and if, as we have good reasons to hope, we should win the election, we should very much like to see you as one of the speakers for the autumn semester.

As to the topic of your lecture we might suggest "Pan-Africanism". But of course we welcome any other suggestion for the topic of your lecture.

In case you will accept this invitation we could arrange that you get a chance to meet prominent Norwegian politicians, and contact the Students Associations in other Scandinavian countries to arrange similar meetings there.

As to the date of the meeting, any Saturday (or any other day) between September and Christmas 1967 would suit us well.

We should very much appreciate a reply as soon as possible, and not later than April 15th.

44 students, Rochester University, U.S.A.

24.3.67

We, the undersigned African students at the University of Rochester, recall with vividness, the circumstances surrounding your overthrow as President of the Republic of Ghana, exactly a year ago.

Despite persistent and destructive "post-mortem" examinations by certain narrow-minded and immature political

215

analysts, we on behalf of budding Pan-Africanists, pledge our unswerving loyalty to the cause of Pan-Africanism, which you have so resolutely and defiantly promoted.

Contrary to the deliberately malicious opinion of our critics that our vision of African unity is a mirage, we hold that "UNITY NOW" is the panacea for all the ills that plague our society. We, therefore, urge you to join forces with other progressive African leaders to ensure that this unity which we wholeheartedly seek shall be an immediate historical and physical reality.

Cognizant of the tremendous psychological, political and economic damages inflicted on our African people through overt and covert foreign control, we implore you to join hands with President Sékou Touré, Mobutu, Nasser, Nyerere, Modibo Keita and other deserving African leaders in dealing a death blow at colonialism, neo-colonialism, and all other institutions of foreign domination.

FORWARD WITH AFRICAN UNITY

Acknowledgement of this letter will be highly appreciated Sir.

A Nigerian Engineer and a Liberian Economist, Montreal, Canada.
24.3.67

The writers are two young Africans, a Nigerian Engineer and a Liberian Economist.

We have both completed a tour of Africa (including Ghana) and Europe. In view of certain analyses made of political structures in various African countries, discussions with various African and non-African student groups, the repercussions of the ouster of your Excellency (the rejoicing in certain areas, evidence of the total lack of any respect for the aspirations of the African peoples) we have come to the conclusion that your ouster is a serious set-back of our dream for a better Africa—free from the shackles of imperialism in all its forms.

We are aware of the fact that in order to effect a come back of your Excellency, many hurdles are to be cleared. In this direction, you already have the moral support of ourselves and the majority of all unselfishly conscientious African intellectuals we encountered during our tour. We are prepared to render our services for the attainment of our common goal—your return to power in Ghana, and we speak for many.

We will appreciate an acknowledgement at your Excellency's earliest convenience.

Kalubewila, Dehiwela, Ceylon.
31.3.67

I have been a very silent observer and admirer of the sincere and patriotic actions taken by you in the past to free your Motherland and the rest of the African continent from the shackles of imperialism. No doubt your honest and sincere actions were crippled by the stooges of imperialism aided by the stinking C.I.A. It no doubt is crystal clear to patriotic citizens of the Eastern World that the only salvation and correct path to free the African continent from the designing imperialists and their stooges is through the "Sacred Path of Socialism" and that you have chosen the correct path.

It is not surprising that your actions have been termed "Subversive" "Self-centred" and "Corrupt" by the stooges of imperialism. I note with profound regret that the latest move made by you to blast the stooges of imperialism holding sway in your beloved country has been "dashed to the ground" according to the imperialist press, with the help of information obtained from trusted emissaries of yours who have been sent by you for various purposes into your Motherland.

In all sincerity, I a "Black" as the "Whites" prefer to refer to us offer to you my services in any capacity at whatever cost it may be to assist you to stage a "come back", free your Motherland and in the process free the rest of the African continent from the ambitious and designing imperialists.

In conclusion I hope and pray that you will be successful in all your attempts to free the suppressed and misguided masses of the African continent.

May I also state that my services are at your disposal within short notice.

Afro-American, Miami, Florida, U.S.A.
6.4.67

As an American of African descent, I am appalled by the monstrous crimes against humanity being perpetrated by world-dominionist forces which rule us.

There is, obviously, a master plan with time table for the complete economic domination of the world by American-controlled military-industrial combines.

My greatest ambition is to join forces with my revolutionary brothers in the struggle for self-determination. Your cause, I feel, is our cause.

I spent six months in the Congo learning more during that brief tenure than in a life time in white-ruled America about my history—the history of Black People, however diluted our blood.

I should deem it a signal honour to be permitted to link my destiny with yours.

To be certain, I would bring some talents for the unstinting application to the cause. As a pilot and administrator, well practised in office management and machinery (office, that is) and some versatility in basic weaponry (small arms), I feel confident that there is a place for me in the active struggle before us.

I beg your indulgence in favouring me with your advice at the soonest date convenient.
P.S. My experiences in local, national and international politics strengthens my convictions.
Nigerian student, Hamburg, W. Germany.
13.4.67

Long ago I had intended to write to you requesting for a help. The political events of a year ago slowed my action. Before I go on with this letter I should like to introduce myself personally to you. I was born in Eket town in Calabar Province in Southern Nigeria. I had lived in Ghana during and after the struggle for independence under your able leadership. It was a memorable occasion. When I returned to Nigeria, I worked in the left wing Trade Union Movement for seven years before being sent to study modern languages three years ago in Eastern Germany, (N.T.U.C.).

I left that country because the combination of languages

that I wanted to study did not exist in their Universities. After living here in West Germany for some time, I am completely fed up with these people as a whole. The same thing applies to my friend, a Ghanaian student. We were together in Leipzig. He left because of the political situation created by the present idiots in Accra. We shall be very grateful if you can recommend us to the Soviet Union preferably the Moscow State University where we can continue our studies.

Your temporary departure from Ghana has left a great political vacuum in African politics. You have more supporters now among those at Accra fighting the imperialists alone. You have shaken the myth of anti-communism in Africa. The reactionary governments in Africa have now been exposed as the real enemy of the black man. I have heard that books have been burnt in Accra. These people cannot destroy your work. During the time of Hitler the same method was applied against authors who were non-Nazis.

After the disappearance of Hitler and his gangsters from the political scene of Germany, these books came up again in great numbers. The American imperialists have sworn that they will never live to see Africa go communist as if Africa belongs to them. Whether these fools like it or not "the wind of change" blowing through Africa will not pass any stooges by. If the Africans had taken your words, there would not have been a second South Africa again. It seems to me that there may be a substantial reason why some Africans in East and Central Africa are so passive on questions concerning the oppressed peoples of that continent.

Those so-called leaders of Africa who did not want to support your views on the question of a continental armed force or a union government did so because they had been wasting their time while they were students. If one has not mastered one's subjects while a student, when can one do it then?

All true sons and daughters of Africa are anxiously looking forward to that great day when you shall return to Accra and continue your task. In spite of all humiliation, I hope you will not be discouraged for we shall soon come to join you in our life struggle.

May I wish you all the best of luck and good health.

Ghanaian Journalist, Ibadan, Nigeria.
17.4.67

I can no longer go on hiding within myself without declaring my dedication for you.

Due to circumstances connected with your absence from home I am now also exiled from home and have now relinquished my Ghanaian nationality. It was my primary intent, when I left home about three months ago to come over to you in Conakry, however due to the absence of my travelling papers and the security around your well-being, I reconsidered my decision and came over to my uncle here. Each day that I have lived here, I have felt additional humiliation and a sense of hopelessness, or rather uselessness, in remaining dormant to the furtherance of the cause which you champion and for which we have given up our lives. Believe me Sir, it is not me alone for there are others of my acquaintance who for their belief have left home for fear of persecution.

I am a journalist, and until you were rebelled against, I was an employee of the Ghana Broadcasting Corporation and in fact was on duty that night when the ungrateful soldiers—some of which were nonentities at school and owe their position to you, came over and made us surrender.

Presently, I have nothing doing and practically cannot write, for without moral force of my belief I cannot bring myself to be a hypocrite, like others whom I knew and during your presence, wrote and spoke like they had some measure of sincerity in them.

My only crime, for which I had to stay in cells for ten weeks at the Special Branch, was that I wrote an article giving my candid opinion about the rebellion. Fortunately enough there was not enough, no! there was no decree to convict me, so by habeas corpus filed in for me I was released.

Honoured Sir, sincerely, my whole life is at your disposal and I do not price anything more precious than the wish to be with you. I have been prompted to write all this for my awareness that to come over without your knowledge and travelling papers, will be well nigh suspicious and perhaps will

220

have to spend some time in custody.

Despite the fact that the present press at home have been screaming about things going good, on my honour Sir, I say things are bad, very bad indeed. As the days pass I become more than ever convinced that there is bound to be another bloody revolution, this time those ungrateful soldiers will have to answer, when the people of Ghana realise their folly. Even now, as I speak, I can call to mind a hundred names of those who do think like I do and will give up all they have to be by your side.

Dear Sir, again I plead my request to be by your side, at your service. For no matter how small my part will be, at least I shall die contented that I did my part.

Hoping to hear from you, I remain, Sir.

Ghanaian student, W. Germany.
3.5.67

I don't have to write much about the state of affairs in our dear Ghana to-day, because, without doubt, you have a true picture of everything.

The poor, less educated Armed Forces and the Police, in their own bid to ameliorate things in Ghana, have clearly demonstrated to the whole world their incapability to do so. Every situation, under greedy Ankrah and his foolish capitalist associates, has been worsened and Ghanaians, for that matter, are now wary of the military rule. Public opinion shows, honestly, that the flames of our confidence in you are now very much aglow.

As for the students abroad whom you fed very well, it is perhaps not necessary for me to talk about the way they think about you, for they have been demonstrating their loyalty to you. Many students, including myself, would return home after our courses only when you have gone back to take upon your shoulders once more, the task of ruling the state of Ghana.

Being one of the many young men who are very loyal to you, I have left home to pursue a course in politics with the hope that I may give a helping hand in your administration.

I wish you all the best of luck, long life and prosperity. C.P.P. will live for ever and ever.

African student, Derby, England.
30.5.67

CAN AFRICA BE UNITED?

I have just read the commentary on the fate of the O.A.U. on its 4th Anniversary—a fading dread—and the best demonstration to the world of the lack in Africa of any feelings for togetherness and unity.

At this time when you must be wondering whether all that you have lived for, the high ideals that you have always stood for on behalf of the African people and the gospel that you tried to hammer home into African thinking are crashed to bits, I consider it my duty to write to you and tell you that in many parts of Africa and the world at large exist many young men whose dreams were crashed with your downfall. One hopes that one day Africa will realise where she is and what a pathetic picture she now portrays to the world. What can the little nations of black Africa do in themselves with their childlishly-clung-to sovereignties, for themselves or even for Africa?

That African personality you once portrayed, that African image which was once very clear in the minds of almost every young thinking African I met, and spoke to, now seems a nice dream that must be forgotten because it is too painful to think that that dream shall never materialise.

It is my strong feeling and I know I am not alone, that your return to Ghana and to the African political scene is a necessity to the entire black African population and I, every day, hope that I will read in the papers—"Nkrumah Once More Head of Ghana"—a dream I myself would like to contribute to its materialising only if I knew how—but one thing I do know—the message you sent in your work, speeches and literature did sink into your African hearts and still lives.

Sometimes I wonder who is to blame now that Africa is not only divided, but quarrelling amongst itself, but whatever you do, do not give up your dreams and ambitions, because the ideals you stood for in themselves are very much worth living for and they can survive the storms of mockery long after their originators are long gone. The question I always ask myself is "What is the destiny of the

little states of black Africa and for how long must they submit and condescendingly open out their arms and appeal for sympathy, aid, etc. from their white contemporary states —how can this everlasting humiliation be checked?"
P.S. I do not have to be an intellectual to feel strongly for the Unity of Africa.

INDEX